HELLO I'LL BE STEALING FROM YOU TODAY

HEATHER SOL

© 2015 by Heather Sol

All rights reserved. No portion of this publication may be reproduced, stored in a retrieval system, or transmitted by any means—electronic, mechanical, photocopying, recording, or any other—except for brief quotations in printed reviews, without the prior written permission of the publisher.

Editors: Christian Pacheco, Kayte Middleton, Hunter Brown, Sarah Miller
Cover Design: Jason Kauffmann / Firelight Interactive / firelightinteractive.com
Interior Design: Book Design and Typesetting / bookdesignandtypesetting.com

Indigo River Publishing
3 West Garden Street Ste. 352
Pensacola, FL 32502
www.indigoriverpublishing.com

Ordering Information:
Quantity sales: Special discounts are available on quantity purchases by corporations, associations, and others. For details, contact the publisher at the address above.

Orders by U.S. trade bookstores and wholesalers: Please contact the publisher at the address above.

Publisher's Cataloging-in-Publication Data is available upon request.

Library of Congress Control Number: 2015956755

Sol, Heather
ISBN: 978-0-9962330-5-7

Printed in the United States of America

First Edition

With Indigo River Publishing, you can always expect great books, strong voices, and meaningful messages. Most importantly, you'll always find . . . words worth reading.

"This work is dedicated to those who recognize all their parts,
the good, the bad, the secret.
Those who can admit fault and who try not to
judge others too harshly.
Let go of mistakes, forgive . . .
Listen. Live. Learn.
And to love, big huge important life changing love.
To you, Alijah Sol."

anxiety girl

1

"All my life my heart has sought a thing I cannot name."
—Hunter S. Thompson, quote from a long-forgotten poem

I'm a frantic walking panic attack, agoraphobia billboard girl. This innate, almost constant anxiety takes me from a young, curious girl into a borderline insane ballerina, deranged debutante, almost actress . . . always anxious. This anxiety comes into my life and steals time away from me, saying "Hello girl, here I am . . . your copilot."

I grew up in small-town southern Louisiana, where almost everyone is close to family and rarely leave the town they are from. Many people here are alike in many ways, being brought up essentially the same. Values are passed down to generations without question of right or wrong, agree or disagree—it just . . . IS. There is a lot of love for those close, and a lot of intolerance for outsiders. Growing up here I often feel a pull, a need to get out, to go out into the world and explore. This is not a feeling many people I know share with me, they are fine here. I often daydream about my family moving to a new state so I get to be a new person in a new place. I have many cousins and friends and am happy much of the time when I'm with them. As I grow up into a preteen, I get more restless and bored. I also feel anxious much of the time and I keep that to myself. It's confusing to me. As I graduate from high school at the age of seventeen, I notice I am not the same as others here. I am not content.

Anxiety is one of my first memories as a young person. I

HELLO I'LL BE STEALING FROM YOU TODAY

remember casually chatting with a few friends and suddenly losing my ability to talk, unable to catch my breath. I can't name what was happening to me or even explain it. I'm outside of myself watching the conversation take place, and then suddenly, I feel weak, unable to keep it together. I run to the bathroom and just say I'm not feeling well. That was my first panic attack. I had no idea then how many of these I would have throughout my life or how many ways I would come up with to explain them away.

Some things, other things, can't be explained away though, even with my anxiety as a reason for it all. All the things you do in life will follow you until the day you die. This means the good, the bad, and the hideous. I am now stuck thinking of things better left in the corners of my mind—terrible, hurtful things I did to my family and myself without a second thought. These events would contain multiple episodes of anxiety and panic during the time I spent running away and for years after. I can hold onto guilt for an amazing amount of time.

A little over ten years ago, in the late '90s right after high school ended, I decided to get out of the small town I lived in, even if that meant running away and never looking back. As an eighteen-year-old curious delinquent, I thought it would be possible to lie, steal, and run away from my problems. So, I enlisted my boyfriend, Xander, at the time, also a curious delinquent, to take to the highway with me on a trip courtesy of my parents' "borrowed" credit card. He had no direction in life either, and he was ready to get away. The only way I ever would have done this trip is with a partner in crime, and no one else would have ever thought it was a good idea except for him.

Some of my problems stemmed from the fact that I was being investigated for stealing money from some small-town, hillbilly office job I had been working at for a few months.

I worked in the office on the days I could pull myself out of bed, answering phones, making appointments, the usual office shit. I often didn't show up for work, or I came in still drunk. I must have reeked like a fucking bar. Most days, I didn't get over the night before until about 2 p.m., but I made sure to go out again that night. My miserable self was under the impression that I was free and life was fan-fucking-tastic. I assume the owners of the company decided that since I was a fuck up anyhow, they would go ahead and charge me with theft. They may have even thought I stole the money. I don't really know.

To avoid these long workdays and the pending charges coming my way, Xander and I hit the highway, and we had no idea where we were going. We'd figure that out once we just got out of dodge. I assumed this bullshit attempt at charging me for this crime would quickly blow over.

As an almost adult, I was always amazed at how utterly clueless I was as to my future plans. People around me seemed to have ideas, plans, things they were working toward—yet here I was just feeling lost. How did I end up this way? I had the same education as my peers, family, friends, and a life that resembled normal, but I somehow came out the wrong door. The others seemed to have more direction. How could I get that? What could I do?

Some just wanted to get married and have babies . . . not for me. A few were already pregnant or had kids . . . good luck with that!

Some were ready for college and already picked out majors. I was ready for college, but only to party and to be independent, free of any rules.

There were a few who had jobs right out of school. No thanks! Call me in twenty years when you hate your life.

Some of the people I knew were going to trade school, to

literally learn a trade and enter the job force eagerly in the next two years. This sounded a lot like hell to me.

Military—I just laugh to myself.

So, I decided I was not a fully developed person. And I was okay with it. Mostly because I had no choice but to be okay—it was where I was.

As I rode down the interstate, I wasn't aware of what awaited me outside that small town and how it was going to take me down quite a few scary paths, some of which I will always regret and a few I will accept as a part of me. I am flawed, in a different way than most of the people around me, but the flaws will at least prove to allow for some adventure!

2

As we left our small town and got on the interstate, it is exciting! It feels great to be away from home and on a journey. I am finally seeing the United States, and it is a sight to behold! Well . . . besides Texas taking up too much time because it's huge and because I happen to lose my stolen credit card. Needing a night out, we go to a small local club. We are watching a bad standup comedy show. I give my credit card to the bartender to open a tab. We have a drink or two, and when it is time to close out the tab, the credit card is gone! The bitch gave it to another customer, who did not notice, signed, and left with my card. My heart sinks, we are now stuck. No card, no money. The manager apologizes and tells us to have a few drinks, that the other customer may come back. Yeah, okay.

Late night at the comedy club waiting for them to return with my card. Free drinks? Thanks, stupid fucks. What last name could possibly even resemble my family name, the common Louisiana last name Arceneaux, in West-Texas nowhere? The bartender was in charge of two credit card tabs, yet she couldn't keep track!? The other customer does not return, and eventually I cannot take being in this place anymore. Back to the hotel to try to figure out what to do next . . .

No choice but to get back on I-10 and drive the eight hours back to where it all began. After speaking to managers at Visa for hours, I finally get them to agree to overnight a new card but only to the original address on the account, my parents' house. It is time to wake up at the ass-crack of dawn and drive there. Yes, I kind of know what time mail

HELLO I'LL BE STEALING FROM YOU TODAY

and FedEx arrive after years of living there, but timing it out just right is going to be difficult. My parents both work, so I know they are not home.

After a long, long drive, we make it to my parents' house within an hour of the expected delivery time for FedEx. I have a key, but I know I wasn't going inside the house considering I may be wanted. So we just sit outside on the back patio waiting. This is a strange feeling, being at the empty home where I grew up—so many memories, good and bad. Part of me wants to just crawl into my bed like a child and hope this is all just a bad dream. But the rest of me knows this whole thing has gone too far, and I have no choice but to continue. What other option do I have? It is over. My parents have written me off. They must have. By now I still have charges pending from my last job, and now I have taken their credit card. I look fucking guilty, I am guilty.

Finally, coming down the quiet country road is that FedEx truck. I make busy work in the front yard until he drives up, so it doesn't look odd that I am meeting him outside.

Oh, hey, FedEx! Yes, thank you. Sign here? Okay. Have a great day!

Knowing my grandparents live three houses down the street and my aunt's house is across from them has made this risky and makes me more aware of the gravity of this situation. I feel like a criminal and know this is not right. I'm a child. Legally an adult, but I am thinking and acting like a child. Someone, notice this!

Seriously, nobody notices—not my family, who live in the neighborhood or even the neighbors, who have known me my entire life. The police are supposed to be watching me, following my every move via that credit card . . . and here I am driving right back where it all began to start over again, getting a replacement credit card. No one is paying any attention.

Before leaving home again, I think how much I wanted to just throw myself at my parents' feet and beg for mercy. Tell them how it all began so simple. I just thought I could leave town for a while while the work charges are resolved, go on an adventure, and then come home and apologize. Or hopefully just get the credit card bill from the mailbox before them and pay it back. But this idea has taken a life of its own now, and I feel like I can't just stop—not right now. I am too far into the bullshit, and I am just too afraid to say how afraid I really am. I am afraid of everything, leaving and staying.

I think of a church group weekend retreat I had taken just a year before. I was ready at that moment for something or someone to help put me on a path of good. Never religious, I was fully affected by that weekend, I saw photos of myself after, and I was glowing! I looked happy, lit from within. Now when I catch a glimpse of myself . . . no light, no happiness left. Just emptiness.

Leaving is my only answer. I am sure they already know. I am already going to jail for this, and I'm so sure they are pressing charges against me, so how can I trust them? I have betrayed them. I just have no idea what I was doing. I have no coping skills.

Most days during my little adventure, I am so anxious I suffer from what I believe are "liar's headaches." I rarely enjoy myself besides the freedom of the open road, going state to state, seeing the Pacific Ocean, moments when I can feel like a kid again. You know, just taking in the beauty of it all. But these moments are few and far between, and I am just running from myself.

How can I be this bad (for lack of a better word) person and who I really feel like I am at the same time? I am not bad. I have been a good daughter, and the hardest part is that I have always loved my parents so much, even now. Since I was a child, I would have dreams of dying or one of my parents dying, and one or all of us would come back to earth with another family. And that shook me. It made me fear daily life and wonder if it was worth living at times. This scared me so much as a young child and I cried. These are other ways anxiety creeps into the brain, causing repetitive scary thoughts to become things to fixate on, to fear. As a teen, these dreams, these thoughts give me panic attacks. I never haven't loved my family. I just don't know how to deal with anything.

So I run.

3

Minor setback now behind us, we got back on the road to wherever we thought acceptable. I still planned on coming back to face the music eventually. I mean, when we left our small apartment, we packed only what was needed, and the rest was put in a storage unit until we came back to Louisiana. But somehow I thought we could just leave for a while with no real consequences. I thought maybe by the time I came home things would be different. I would be found innocent of the charges, and then maybe I could pay my parents back and move on. It would be difficult but we would work it out because they would know how afraid I was, understand why I ran.

We headed toward Kansas, mostly because I had family there who might be willing to help me out with getting a job or getting into school. My thinking was that if I could get my shit together while I was away, then when I returned, things would be better. When we arrived in Kansas and checked into another hotel room paid for by my parents' credit card, I called home to check in and see if there were any suspicions of my absence. I was still unsure if they knew I had left town, or if they knew about the credit card I was using. I had just moved into my first apartment away from home, and still going to their home much of the time. Usually we would speak daily, so I was sure they suspected something.

My dad answered and asked me where I was, and immediately I knew they knew. He said my mom was at my aunt's house and to call her there. I called her but did not tell her where I was, though I later found out they had traced the call and knew where I was.

HELLO I'LL BE STEALING FROM YOU TODAY

She said she knew I was running and wanted me to come home. We both cried, and I really wanted to just tell her everything and go home, but I was scared to go to jail. She believed that I had stolen the money, and that killed me. She spoke to me differently; she felt distant and colder than ever before, and I just knew I would never again have a mother in my life. I was hurt, and I was a child.

I needed someone to save me at that very moment. I figured she knew about the credit card I had, but she did not mention it. I needed her to yell at me, to tell me stop fucking around and get home now, tell me everything would be okay, anything but this mom with a weird voice who didn't seem to care.

I found out later that the police told them to continue to allow me to use their credit card so they could track my location and put me in jail later for more charges. Police should always stay out of family business. They give advice knowing only parts of the story and can often legally fuck over someone for a lifetime, following the law with aggression and anger at times. Police are not coming from a place of love or compassion, were not seeing me as a person.. Pursue the actual charges perhaps, but don't advise my family on how to handle me.

When I hung up the phone, I knew it was time to make some decisions that would put me either on a pathway toward home or on another pathway toward lawlessness. I could no longer call my family in Kansas. They would help my parents and turn me in immediately. I had come all this way for nothing, and I truly felt hopeless. I cried and wanted to slit my wrists that night. I tried to do it, but I was so young and ill-prepared. I wanted to be dead but was so scared and didn't have a clue what to do. I cried and cried until I became angry, put the blade away, and then I chose lawlessness. In my young mind, I had no choice. I was not going to go to jail in that small town that felt like a jail already.

After staying up most of the night in a tiny bathroom, thinking of any possible solution, I awoke the next day with a plan. I knew my parents could fight all of the credit card charges—they were not authorized—so why not use the money and lose the paper trail? I was proud of my little plan though I knew I would have to face my parents eventually.

My partner-in-crime boyfriend and I would drive to a small town where I would walk into banks, not huge banks but small local ones. I would tell the teller I needed to get a cash advance off of the credit card I was using. I would say that it was an emergency, and I did not have my PIN. But, I would say, I am an authorized user on the account. I had no idea if this would work, but I thought it was worth a shot, and all they could say was yes or no.

My idea was that if I could get cash advances, I would ditch the credit card, and they could not track me any longer. The first bank I walked into had only one employee in the front, and she was smiling and nice when I walked in. I immediately thought, "*I got this.*" I kept my explanation simple, telling her I needed cash because I had some bills due and my mom (the cardholder) was in the hospital. She said she had never done that before and made a quick phone call. The person on the other line told her to call the credit card company and verify that I was an authorized user, which she did. I'm not sure what the details of the phone call were, but when she hung up, her next question to me was, "How much cash did you need today?" This was going to be too fucking easy!

I requested $2,000, which she quickly gave to me in hundred and twenty dollar bills. I signed a piece of paper, and I was on my way. I walked out excited and feeling a rush like I had never felt before. I was ALIVE! I got back into the car, and my boyfriend was shocked to find out it had worked. My plan was flawless! We thought it would be a good idea to do this same transaction at another bank before getting rid of the card and taking off without a paper trail.

But as we drove around, it occurred to me that the credit card company may have authorized this deal only to send the police out immediately to arrest me. We talked about it for a while and decided that it may just be true. We had enough money with the $2,000, and the cash we brought on the trip was about $250. We would use that to get to Seattle, where we would stay with friends, get jobs, and rent an apartment. I cut the credit card up into pieces and threw it into a trashcan at a gas station, and we were on our way.

As we merged onto the highway, my high from the bank transaction quickly wore off and I felt lower than I had ever felt before. I had one of those anxiety headaches, and I wanted to die. I thought about taking the wheel and running the car off of a bridge, but I somehow kept my composure. I wanted to go home, but I knew there was no way I could ever go back. I went too far.

4

Our travels took us to Seattle as we had planned, and now my family had no idea where we were. We stayed with friends sometimes, and other times we lived in cheap motels. My life had become empty and I wanted to go home. Being free had come at too high a cost, and now I regretted everything I had done to get here. I felt lower than ever and hoped for death.

Death came in small spoonfuls. The death of my morals came with a job I took as a waitress in a strip club just to survive in the city. It was dirty and low, just like my life, and the tips were shitty because the laws did not permit the sale of alcohol at nudie bars. This meant a bunch of perverts eating popcorn and drinking sodas, and that is a damn sorry sight.

The death of my soul was a work in progress, and in Seattle, I felt like a shell of the person I once was. I lost weight, had nightmares, and I turned to the bottle any chance I got. At this point, even though we were staying with a friend, we could barely afford to eat on my meager income.

One October day, we found ourselves snowed in during an unseasonable snowstorm. We stayed indoors all day, ate ramen noodles, and drank cheap wine. I found my mind drifting to days spent with my family—vacations, holidays, boring Sundays. I longed for these times again, and I wished my family were there with me. I wanted to share this moment, looking at the snowy street, the rooftops of the other houses covered with snow, fireplaces burning.

I suddenly wanted to jump off the roof. Would I die? The house was only two stories, but it sure seemed tall enough from the view I had.

HELLO I'LL BE STEALING FROM YOU TODAY

Suddenly, my boyfriend was there, telling me everyone was going for a walk to play in the snow. I went along and had fun, but my heart was heavy. I felt empty.

We stayed in Seattle for a little under a year. The friend we were staying with in Capitol Hill lived with so many roommates he did not even know some of their names. Some of them were sick of us sleeping on the sofa though, and we had very little money for an apartment. We called some friends of ours in Austin, Texas, and they said we should head that way and stay with them while we looked for jobs and got settled there. Considering Texas was a little more affordable, we agreed. Working to save enough money to get to the next destination, from Seattle to Austin, was difficult. I rarely left work with more than twenty or thirty dollars in my hand waitressing at the strip club, and I was not working every day. It seemed impossible to ever save when we had to eat and pay for our gross, temporary house at the sleazy motel. So we (Well, mostly my boyfriend.) devised a little system of getting free food. It was almost starvation at this point, and we were pretty desperate.

Having little gas money to drive around and try this at different restaurants, I would call right after lunch and say our food was wrong from a take-out order a few hours ago. Often, after a bit of talking, I would get us a meal or two free in replacement of the one we never bought earlier. It was a bit demeaning, but I was no longer my old self and it was better than starving. After a while, we moved to fast food places because I realized you could drive up and say the day manager put a note for your replacement order and you were to pick it up later that evening. Some managers would ask questions, but most would just hand over the little bit of food I was asking for with apologies. This was how we got our meals for a while until I could save for gas money.

At one point, I was picking up yet another replacement order, and the manager came to the window with my food and said, "Look, kid, I know what you're doing, and I feel bad for you. I hope you can get your life together. You are bone thin, and you could be my daughter. It's sad to see such a young girl doing this."

I left crying. I was unsure how to feel. Angry because I was busted and felt guilty or glad someone reached out? Sad was the main feeling, though. Perpetually sad these days.

A little more than two weeks in, I could not take it. This is when I decided we had to go. Austin sounded too good to continue living this way. We could just not pay the motel manager for the next week's stay, then we might have enough to make it to Texas at that point. We had to just leave. And so, we did. Soon we were on the highway again, and as we drove through the redwoods in California, I felt free again. Like this move was the right one.

The two of us stayed in cheap motels during our drive from Seattle to Austin. Gas money holding out, replacement meals all around the U.S., and seeing the world through eyes filled with dread but disbelief—this was my life. I had to live it.

We ate those meals rarely and had some drinks here and there. We got along well, considering we did not know each other that well before we took off on this journey. He seemed like a privileged kid to me, someone with parents who would save his ass if he needed it. Yeah, right. He did not have much money when we left on the trip, and he did not work at all in Seattle. It was my idea to take off on this trip, though, and I assumed by the time we made it to Texas, we would both get jobs.

Every once in a while, I felt a strange sensation, like I could not get enough oxygen. My breaths were shallow, and my body felt weak. Xander helped me through these times, he was patient with me and talked me through the bad times. It was nice to have a partner-in-crime. We were conveniently falling in love, and that isn't a storybook kind of love.

5

I pick up the pay phone to call home—collect call from the daughter you most likely hate. I am somewhere in Montana, and I'm feeling alone and afraid. I think this was a huge mistake, and I want to just drive home and talk to you about it all. Will you listen? Can I tell you what I have really been thinking and feeling all this time?

I am too tired to keep driving, but too afraid to turn around. These places are all very different from home. Though I thought I hated home, there are worse places. All of these small towns we pass through remind me that I am not so different. We were stuck on a mountain in a snowstorm a few nights ago in a town with only one street. We had to sleep in the car because it was snowing so hard we could not drive downhill. We hardly had enough clothes to stay warm and could only turn the heater on in the car when absolutely necessary. I thought that was going to be the night we died.

I saw people in that small town walking home with their families, and it made me so sad. I want you to accept this call so we can talk like family members talk. Not involving cops who don't give a shit about any of us, just talk. I wish I could say all of this before you had to decide if you wanted to accept the collect call. That way I would know that by accepting, we can talk openly and honestly. I am scared. I feel alone. I feel ashamed.

Will you accept the charges for this call?

I hang up the phone without dialing, had just held it for a while. I am going to find a place that will serve alcohol to underage girls.

6

I thought I was alone in my mental struggle growing up, but I really started to look at myself during my cross-country trip.

I seem to really fucking struggle with things that seem to come easily to others.

This has been an issue throughout most of my life. It comes in a wide variety of cruel and unusual forms, and it's almost always the important stuff in life.

The biggest issues involve relationships. I look at things differently than others do as far as I can gather, and from a young age, this made me feel pretty odd. I had a hard time relating to people. Most of them are boring or just make me uneasy, anxious. If I was having a conversation, especially in my younger years, I'd often wonder where to look, how much eye contact is normal, are my responses making sense? Was I even listening? This is anxiety. Question everything.

I could not understand why I rarely gave a fuck about small talk or making new friends. None of that came easily to me, and it made me feel like I was flawed. Even after I made friends with someone, I would hold back, afraid my true self would not be enough or too much. I never really let people know me for fear of rejection. I would ascertain the personality traits they found favorable and be that person as much as I could. Exhausting work.

Then, there was my family. I felt as though I was so very different I could not be from this group. I saw very few qualities in my family that I wanted to emulate. They all seemed very angry much of the time, and I could never figure out why. Were they crazy, as I assumed I was, and tired of it?

We had good times too, of course, and our family was big and pretty close. It was fun when we were happy, so I wondered why we couldn't just be fucking normal happy people. My mom and dad seemed to have no problem ruining a perfectly good time with their intense anger at each other. They seemed to hate each other at times. I think my young mind wanted only the happy moments. I tried to avoid the difficult, tried to stay in the happy or easy for years. But it was all very confusing to me because just when I would start to feel I was opening up, getting closer to them or getting along with everyone, they would shoot me down with, "Why are you so closed off?" or "Why don't you share your life with us, open up more?"

One day, as we were sitting outside having a casual conversation, my mom delivered my own personal favorite knife to the heart when she suddenly informed me that I was "difficult to get close to." What the fuck is that? You're my mother, and I'm your child. How much closer do you want me to get?

She probably didn't mean it as I took it. She may have even worded it differently. But it made me, again, feel like a freak, an oddball. No one can talk to me or like me, not even my family? Great feeling.

So, as self-fulfilling prophecies go, I became that creation. The person no one could get close to.

7

Then came the Wonderful World of Teenage Sexuality for the young female. How cruel, when you suddenly become attracted and attractive to boys, yet you have no clue what to do or how to handle that power. It's not even evident that it's a power. We can just go blindly into fucking guys who don't give a shit about us, assuming it will get them to like us more, when it actually makes them walk away. They got what they want, toots!

Here's a bright idea: we need to do young ladies the honor of speaking to them about their bodies and their personal power. Teach them how to use it and how to find what they really want. So many young ladies feel powerless, as though the guys are in control, when really it's so wrong. We control our own bodies. Tell them that they are better off masturbating and knowing themselves and their bodies before anyone else sneaks or forces their way in. Strip away the bullshit and speak the truth. Many young girls do all the wrong things, not sure what to do with all the sudden male attention, you know, what feels like love.

I did what my friends were doing. I went for it. I wanted to have sex, and high school seemed to be the time. I was getting older, so after high school I found my group of crazy, deranged nut bags in the slightly larger town just twenty-five minutes away from my small, boring town. Here is where I went to bars, made new friends, found my people. I had a good girl friend who also lived in my small town, Opelousas, and also loved to drive the short distance to find our people in the dive bars of "the strip," as it was called. We were a good team.

We both soon found new boys to hang out with, some that would stick around for a weekend or two, nothing serious. Hers was an interesting guy who seemed bisexual—he was interested in girls but flirted with some of our guys. At the time, metrosexual wasn't a term, but that was also him. I had a new friend of my own. He had a girlfriend, but I didn't give a shit. He was hot, looked like Jesus, who I always found really hot, and he liked to party (my new man, not Jesus). We met through a mutual friend who owned one of the bars, and I was a smitten kitten. I think he was selling drugs though, so he ended up in jail, and I ended up very sad. My first really good lay—a huge partier—in jail for a long time. Then again, a lot of people in our group sold drugs. He just got caught, which was bad for me. I was picky, and he was hot!

I quickly moved on. I don't even think I wanted to have sex the first few times. I think I just thought I was supposed to want to. Honestly, I found it pretty gross, as I do most things having to do with the human body. It was awkward, too. Who knew what to do? Not me, but I could pretend. And that's what I did: pretend I was mature, ready, willing, whatever. It wasn't a big deal. Until it was.

The first time I was raped, it was quick and disgusting, and I felt helpless and stupid for flirting with and then going home with an older guy. He said we were going to his house for something, I don't know what. I rode there with him.

I blamed myself. He kissed me with his thin lips and pointy tongue. He tasted like tooth decay. I did not like it, but I also did not want to be rude. In some stupid way, I never wanted to be rude. I pushed him away after the second kiss, but he became forceful. He barely took off his pants, and he attacked me for his own pleasure. I cried, and I remember thinking that at least his disgusting dick was small and it was over soon.

He was an adult. I was a child. I blamed myself. I told

no one. Even though I would see him at a mutual friend's house now and again, I never ran errands with him again and started hating my body. It nauseated me just to see him. He acted like it was no big deal, though, like we were friends. I felt like I was attracting this negative attention.

The second rape was extraordinarily violent. He hit me and hurt me and did so much shit to me for so many hours that I can't even remember it all. He heard my cries and my screams, and I could see he liked it. It was a turn-on. I was sure he would kill me. I was dating him, and I had no fucking idea what was wrong with me.

I would block both incidents out for a long time, remembering them at the same time right at the peak of my worst anxiety and depression. Right when I was trying to decide how to end my life, these memories would come back to me like little fucked up mental gifts. That was when I thought about suicide by gun to the vagina. But, let's not get ahead of ourselves.

I think my anxiety stems from many things, and my disgust of people comes from my anxiety. But these childhood difficulties, labels, expectations, all of those have fed the beast within. Not having anyone understand me or having anyone to talk to just gave these people chances to use my body and hurt me forever.

Later, I would find drugs. A new way to hurt myself and abuse my body, this time by my own hands. I felt like it gave me some control, as twisted as that sounds. I liked to get fucked up. I hoped I would fall into a deep, deep sleep.

8

Back in my car . . . Somewhere, driving down these United States interstates on the road to nowhere, I decided to check out mentally. Maybe not a conscious decision, but my brain had enough of going over and over what I could have done differently. My emotions were all over the place, usually very low, and I was exhausted. I had to let myself live a bit, so I checked out from my normal way of thinking and feeling. I became numb, feeling very little pleasure or pain with daily life but also letting go of the brain commotion that was constantly going on. When I gave into this feeling, I resigned myself from family relationships in my own way. To better deal, I put it away. The thing about trying to put too much away is eventually it comes spilling out, making a huge mess.

Once I let go, I did see the journey as having some purpose. You don't just travel three fourths of the U.S. without learning a few things. I was young, but along the road, I had grown up a bit and was more aware of what I had done and the hurt I had caused. I wanted to have been able to take this journey under different circumstances. I wished I had the family that would have said, "Go take a trip. College will be there."

I picked up on little things about my own personality I had not noticed before. I was longing to give to others in some way. Besides my tendency to try to please people, I don't know if I ever knew this about myself. I learned a lot about compassion and to try not to judge others. I found that I could be a very loyal friend to people, some I just met. I wasn't a bad person in spite of some things I did; maybe my family would see that.

But I also learned a lot of hard lessons about life. It's not easy to be out of the safety of close family and friends. It's really scary to feel so alone so far away from home. If making it on my own meant starting from nothing, I was not so sure I was into it. I enjoy creature comforts and just relaxing at times. Being home in my pajamas with my family watching a movie could sound like heaven to me even when I was deep in the redwoods enjoying beautiful views and seeing parts of the world I may never see again. Thinking about where my next meal was coming from was a disgusting low, and I was there far too many times—had been there when trying to get the money for Austin.

At one point before leaving Seattle, very low on funds, I walked into a very shady-looking motel in a row of shady-looking motels to ask about a rate—a horrible place full of sad, dazed faces. I smelled the place before I was completely through the door. It smelled like raw eggs, smoke, death.

Everyone's here for their own reasons. I can't judge. I'm here, too.

It was dirty and plain. I think that it's a sign of my future if I keep living this way. Dirty and ashamed, running all the time and getting nowhere. It felt like pure hell, walking into that shabby lobby, curtains faded from years of hanging in dust on the filthy windows, a smoking man behind the small desk. I saw what seemed to be a hooker outside, starting to walk around the lots of these disgusting motels. It was one of the lowest days I had faced at that point. After talking to Mr. Two Teeth, I found that we could stay there for a week or two while I tried to make money waitressing at the strip club down the street.

Working the day shift with murder-minded crazies in yet another Northern strip club—not fun like Southern "eggs and legs" or buffet lunch strip clubs with cocktails, where meetings take place for major oil company owners. This club had legit crazies. The pale faces sitting in the dark in the middle of the day eating popcorn and drinking soda, they stared at the fully nude strippers and always sat alone.

Not many groups here, not a fun place. The pole in this lovely club had to be wiped down every now and then, not after each completely naked girl, just when they played this one break song. Staff knew it was time to grab the towel and clean the gross pole . . . Time to clean the pussy pole, lowlife workers!

Of course, I applied for work just about anywhere else—cafes, restaurants, all that. But it was just easier to get into these clubs because girls didn't last long, so I just moved from one to the next, feeling desperate. Time was running out.

It never occurred to me to get pissed at my traveling companion for not looking harder for work. I was in survival mode, and all I had was him to keep me sane. Otherwise, I was out there alone.

9

Later in life, I learned a few new things about myself that helped me better understand the overwhelming anxiety I live with. I can hear things people say in the most negative, judging, accusatory tone possible. It's why it took a long time to feel comfortable around my own family. If they said something I could find negative connotation to, I could internalize it so completely it would devastate me for days. It was always hard to explain, so instead I just went through those days silent, always feeling judged, like the things I did wrong were not a big surprise because I was always a fuck up. This is a message I may get from a simple conversation with my mother. Now, my mom could just be focusing on something else that day and unable to give her attention. It could be something so simple, but I would take that as an attack, a sneaky attack, cleverly planned to make me feel like shit. It's hard to relate to people when you are always assuming the worst in conversations.

In therapy, sometimes therapists do this exercise where one person will say a sentence to the other person about the way they are feeling. Then, the person will say "What I heard was . . ." and attempt to say what they heard from that comment. This would have been interesting to do back then with my family and me. May have been fun or helpful—before. I bet I could have surprised everyone with what I could ascertain from a single comment. When I was still there, still trying to communicate with people. Not shutting everyone out and hiding inside my home, hardly able to face anyone.

10

To really get to know someone's personality, psychologists, psychiatrists, and therapists look into a patient's past to heal the wounds of the past and move forward. You have to know yourself. Identify why and when did I become this way—this is often what patients are searching for.

But the focus is largely on parental relationships and how those have affected growth. But I have started to see a big correlation between who we are and why we do what we do in looking at sibling relationships.

Most families have working parents who come home exhausted and feel like they have little to give. If the household has more than one child, it's often the kids who start to parent each other, and the younger ones watch and learn from the older. While the parents are busy, the oldest becomes the new role model for the younger kids. This is sometimes great. There are older sibling family units where the younger kids benefit from the oldest, grounded, calm, and loving sibling.

But when this dynamic is out of balance and everyone involved is unaware of that fact, it can get fucked for the younger. If there are two sisters, close in age who are left alone much of the time and that older girl is nuts, it's going to get weird. It's hard to know who is right and who to listen to when you grow up with people so different from you. Parents mean well, but don't yet know you. The older sister sees she has a bit of power and uses it.

Things happen between siblings that parents don't know about.

HELLO I'LL BE STEALING FROM YOU TODAY

I watched my older sister go after guys, relationships, like her life depended on it. When it came to relationships, no one else mattered. They were her air. She was much more focused on getting a boyfriend than having girlfriends to the point where she would step on a friend's face to try to take her guy and not think twice about it. It wasn't normal. This is where I first rebelled against the idea of having to have a boyfriend in my life. From a young age, I knew that something was not right with that type of behavior. To me, it seemed like way too much work for relationships that mostly ended up unhappy.

But my older sister would feed children to wolves to please the man who was currently using her. Later in life, she fed her own children to the metaphorical wolves. She was being used then, too. That relationship led to another one, again longterm, again unhealthy. She will always throw her family away in a second to please these men. Looking back now, I think it was an issue of codependency. My sister has so much good about her, but it seemed like she got more out of life with negative action.

So, even as a kid, I tried my best not to be like her, especially when it came to relationships. I wanted friends, to travel—to be free. This is the opposite of having a boyfriend in a small town because he would most likely stay in that small town. I also saw an odd thing in these guys: they wanted a version of their own mothers. Gross. They wanted to move out of Mommy's home, get married, and have a "wifey mommy." These wifey mommies will do all the things the guys' moms did: cook, clean up after him and the kids, take care of all the responsibilities in the home, raise the kids, bring his freaking dinner to him because he is too lazy to get the fuck up. But then she'll also give him a blowjob after clearing the table, fuck him when he says so, and will not worry about her orgasm, just his. This is an actual situation I have heard about repeatedly. It made me want to run away and never look back.

Then there was the very little human emotion my older sister showed. The only thing I think she can really feel is envy. Any other emotion seems foreign to her. Her indifference made me so angry I often just wanted to punch her. She didn't seem to feel much of anything. Unkind to animals but will talk to someone she hardly knows in this very fake way and then walk away hating them. The crazy show came out of her face.

She had a boyfriend when we were young, she in high school and, me in seventh and eighth grade. He had no personality, hardly even spoke, and I never got much of a feeling that he had a pulse. Boring as hell.

One day, we were in his car coming home from school, and I was in the backseat. He was driving super slowly down our street, and when I complained, he went slower. At one point, the car was hardly moving at all. I could see my house and said I was getting out. I'd had enough of both of them.

Well, when I opened my door and told him again, "I'm getting out of the car," he kept rolling slowly. The minute my right foot hit the road, I felt the tire creeping up on top of it. Being flexible, I moved my body so I would not break my knee and felt the weight of this stupid little car sitting on top of my foot, the inside of my foot grinding against the pavement. Both sides felt like they were going to fucking crack open.

I yelled to Mr. Personality, "You are on my foot!" I have no clue if he even knew what I was saying, but he didn't really speed up or try to help even as I was screaming loud as fuck. That car just kept creeping over my foot, the ankle turned at a very odd angle, and my body was falling on the road to keep the weird angle so I would not snap my foot off. When the car was finally off of me, I got up and limped over to my house, crying and confused. Neither of them checked on me, helped me, nothing! They acted like I was overreacting or something.

I went inside, in pain and in shock. My foot was destroyed. The side that took the weight of the tire was already bruised, and I could not move it. The side that was smashed into the road was a mess, skin was in pieces inside of my sock, there was blood, and so much skin had come off! I remember being nauseated at the amount of skin inside of my sock, just peeled from my foot. I was afraid, but my sister was not afraid for me. She did not ask me how I was but said it would be okay, that it wasn't broken. She said I needed to keep this between us, not tell our parents.

I need to go to the hospital!!!

She told me no, I didn't need to go to the hospital, and that if I said anything, our parents would be mad at her stupid boyfriend and mad at me for trying to get out of a moving car.

I felt confused, still in shock, and remembered telling him I was getting out of the car. He should have stopped moving. But it was her, so dismissive and aloof. It was as if I had a splinter or something. I needed medical attention! I was already unable to walk—what was I supposed to do about ballet class? Her answer was to say I twisted it in PE at school. It would be okay.

I cleaned it myself while she went on with her afternoon. I cried. It hurt. It looked pretty crazy, purple and black on one side, bleeding and shedding skin on the other. I felt that it was my fault because both of them made it seem that way. Neither of those two cold fucks checked on me, and no one apologized or tried to help me clean this wound. It was turned on me, my problem. I had to deal with it. It took months to heal.

It took years for the bruising to go away, and many years later in the right light, I can still see both injuries' outlines.

I was dismissed by a person who was supposed to take care of me. My sister and I were together a bunch, but there were very few times I felt she cared for me. I kept trying to see some good in her, wanted to believe she loved me. She was kind to me when it suited her needs. When I became friends with her second boyfriend, she wanted to know everything, wanted to be my friend. I thought it was real at the time, but once I started to focus on her and try to get closer to her, she pulled away.

There were times I knew how fake she was being to our own parents, but I couldn't say anything. They seemed to like her better—especially my dad—and they seemed to think she was a good person. This left me wondering where I fit in, wondering what the fuck a good person was.

I did not fit in. I could not say anything. She had our parents fooled. I was the outsider.

She used me so many times with our parents. I took the blame or hid things I knew I should have spoken up about. Her feelings were not there. She was vacant.

Being left with her after school while our parents both worked can maybe be somewhat to blame for my confusion and rebellion. Therapists go to the parents, but so much time is spent out of their earshot. Luckily, I had a couple of best friends and a very close cousin growing up. I could go to their homes and get a very different perspective on life and people.

I just knew it felt wrong, her energy, her way of thinking, so I wanted to be her complete opposite. And we are opposites in so many ways. But I wonder if maybe I had a different sibling or multiple siblings or just none at all . . . I wonder if my running away from that small town would have been so quick, if it would have been under the same circumstances. I don't doubt I would have left that place eventually. I hated it. But I wonder if I had more emotional guidance from someone I respected, if that would have made a difference.

I was running from my life, getting away from everything and everyone, but it was my sister who showed me how to be cold, how to cut people out of my life.

I tried it too, during my ride across the U.S. I thought I was going to never talk to my family again. It's great to know I couldn't do it. I could not be like her.

I love.

I don't have a huge circle of people I want in my life, but the ones I love are always my priority. And I'm honest. If I don't like you I won't pretend. I have seen that. It's ugly.

11

Austin, Texas was an okay place to be—better than Seattle—but I missed my family and wanted to go home. We had lived there for about six months, and I was still the one working to cover the bills while Xander did not work. I figured that would change, and he would find work too. I assumed that often, and he told me he looked for work, but nothing came of it.

I missed my family and friends, and it was almost time for Mardi Gras, so we decided to make a trip back home. I had to attempt penance for my sins. I knew I had charges and warrants, but I didn't really know what they were for. I was tired of feeling hopeless and I wanted to be able to exist without paranoia.

The night we came into Louisiana, it was already late, after 10 p.m. Since I couldn't talk to my family at that time of night, we decided to go out to one of our favorite bars for some drinks and talk to old friends. We had a good night, and I felt good about being there. I was going to face up to the credit card charges, the fleeing, and whatever happened between my parents and me, hoping it could be better. Sometime during the night, we were given a small baggie of cocaine by an old friend. Xander and I snorted a little of it and then put it in my purse to give it to the friend we were spending the night with that night. At 2 a.m. when the bars were shutting down, we went to the car. Nearby, we saw a cop interrogating, really grilling some girl about something; about what, I had no idea. Poor girl.

Xander drove, I sat in the passenger's seat, and our friend J was in the back. We pulled out the cocaine, and J dumped it onto a big vanity mirror I had in the back seat. The little that was left in the baggie was put back into my purse. I used a razor to cut lines for the three of us. I was so drunk I could hardly see straight. I caught a glimpse of myself in the mirror, and again I looked and felt like a different person. As we pulled into the parking lot of J's apartment, suddenly we were surrounded by police cars and lights.

There were at least five cop cars around us immediately. I cursed and yelled and tried to put the mirror under the seat of the car. I thought they were here for J. He was always in trouble. I asked him, "What the fuck did you do?"

He didn't seem to know, but thought they were there for him also. Xander took the keys out of the ignition, and we all placed our hands up like the cop on the loud speaker asked us to do. Then the cop said something shocking: "Ms. Heather, get out of the car slowly and place your hands behind your back."

What the fuck? They were here for me? I was scared and a little relieved. I did what I was told, and when I stepped out of the car, there was a cop to cuff me. I cried and screamed as he put me in the back of the police car and asked me where my ID was. I told him it was in my purse, and he went to my car to grab it. They let the guys go, but confiscated the car keys since my parents had reported the car stolen.

Really, the cops had gotten lucky, as I would find out. Someone had hit my car while trying to park and then attempted to leave, but a police officer saw and went over to the driver. He ran both license plates and found out I was wanted for months. He then harassed the girl driving the other car, asking her if she knew me. He got lucky, and called for backup. He was taking down a ninety-five-pound fugitive girl—send in the troops!

We were soon on our way to the police station. Tomorrow was Mardi Gras, I was drunk, handcuffed, and afraid. I was only nineteen years old. I realized at that moment that it was my dad's birthday—and that I would kill myself.

12

I am sitting in jail, just woke up from a fifteen-hour nap. Sleep is the only way I can cope. I sleep deeply and do not dream. The bed is metal and covered only with a thin, dirty mattress. I have rods in my spine from a scoliosis surgery a few years ago, and it feels like my back is bleeding inside. I have not eaten in two days, and I feel weak. I had a little juice and some water, but I refuse to eat the food in this place. Even though I can leave my cell, I don't, unless I have to get a drink or make a phone call. The other ladies in here are old, and they are criminals. I am afraid to speak to most of them and don't want to because I seek peace and quiet. They keep asking me if I want food, and I say no. I just want sleep. I think about dancing classes when I was young, how much I loved to dance and perform. I think back to camping with my family, and I smile inside. Only for a second, and then the tears come.

My life is truly over, and I know there isn't anything I can do. My parents take my calls, but they refuse to get me out of here unless I go into a drug treatment center. How stupid can they be? Even I know the only reason I do drugs at all is because I feel dead inside.

I feel my breath getting shallow on the third night in jail. It is so bad it keeps me from sleeping, and I sit up in bed. My hands are shaking, and I feel like the walls are closing in on me. I am sweating and freezing, and I cannot get air. I can feel the tremors in my legs and my back. It feels like I am having a slight seizure. I'm going to die here.

I try to take deep breaths, and when I finally get myself

breathing again, my body relaxes a little. When I lay back in bed, I cry like a baby. I cry for everyone I hurt, for myself, for regrets, fear, and I cry for my parents. I need them so badly. I am scared I am going to die. I've gone from wanting to die to fearing real death in just a matter of moments.

13

All that pain began so many years ago . . .

Her youth was what saved her from understanding the true danger and risks of the surgery. At age twelve, she was too young to really know what would happen and how much of an impact it would have on her life, forever. A dancer (mostly ballet) since age three, she was pliable and limber. Bouncing back seemed like it would be easy when she considered it. A year of healing with about four to six months of bed rest. Bed rest sounded like a vacation. She could lay around all summer, watch TV, and get served meals in bed, healing of course, but nothing made it sound very scary.

Even considering the surgery and implantation of rods in the spine, it was okay to her. Doctors do these things all the time, and they know what they are doing. She will lose some of her ability to arch her back and will grow a few inches. The rods will remain in her body forever, making her stronger and better in a way. Her weak back would be fortified with stainless steel rods, and she would feel different, but deal with it.

The scariest parts were the conversations about the things too technical to understand, but the tone was obvious. The doctors talked about degree of curvature and said things like, "The progression is too fast."

Without surgery, she could end up in a wheelchair. That was scary, but that was why they were doing this, to avoid the worst. It was to make her better. But the tone in the room of some of these frantic, and suddenly endless doctor's appointments made it obvious that she was in some sort of danger. What kind or how it would go, she was unsure. But everyone had that look of pity, the one you give to people who you know are in a shitty situation. But usually the conversations would end with a little upbeat talk about how within a year she could be back to her old self, maybe even back in dancing classes—just no horse riding or trampolines. Yeah, okay. Horses are not an issue; they are big and scary, though pretty. Trampolines would come in time.

Her parents would talk about it with her sometimes, but mostly when she was not in the room, and they would whisper and say things she was not supposed to hear. "Risks" was a common word, so her job was to make sure she was strong and not worry them. It would be okay. Her back would heal and all would go back to normal.

A few months later, school ended, and it seemed like a rushed process of getting this surgery to happen. This seemed normal, as healing needed to take place in the summer so she could go back to school in the fall. But there was also the bleak truth that her body was changing, and her spine was moving in an alarming rate. This was talked about after another round of X-rays, endless X-rays. Suddenly it was progressing too fast, so it was time. Now.

Maybe, being young, we block out what we don't want to hear or maybe the details were not really talked about until she was in the hospital. Either way, in the hospital is where the tragic fear took over her. This fear was relentless, and she wanted to run immediately. She knew there were risks, but now suddenly there was too much talk about paralysis, a word she could not bear to hear, a thought she could not even face. The possibility of this occurring suddenly seemed so common. They spoke about it at almost every single pre-surgery meeting. "Risks" was a word that caused immediate and insane fear, making everything else scary. Every move the nurses made to prepare, every paper signed acknowledging this possibility made it too real and too close. She shook and cried at night. Trying to stay strong for everyone and trying not to show how afraid she was became too much.

Surgery would be the next morning—6 a.m. It would last at least six hours. Her young, small body would be cut open and pulled and pushed for six whole hours. This sounded like a long time, a hideous amount of time and possibility to become paralyzed. Sleeping the night before a surgery like this is nothing short of brutal—it's impossible, and it's time standing still and moving too fast all at the same time.

If there was sleep, or if it was simply wakeful dreaming, it was the same story over and over in her head. She woke up from surgery paralyzed. They told her, and she pretended to be okay with it long enough to be left alone with the wheelchair. She wheeled herself to the top of the hospital and threw herself off the roof top. The fall did not hurt, obviously, but it felt like relief from the chance of never walking again at that moment.

Life was about youth, and youth was about movement. How could she go on with a life with no movement and no chances? The dream occurred over and over until time for surgery the next day. It was scary to be rolled into the operating room, but the IV drugs helped a bit. She stayed as strong as possible for the family, who held her hand and walked with her until they were told this was it . . . they had to wait for at least six hours. Once she was through the double doors and away from the family, her strength was gone. She was a crying child being placed into what may be her deathbed. She screamed, and they replied with more meds, kept her rolling toward that room. At some point, the walls were thick and dripping with a kind of painted heat, coming off the wall and closer to her each second. Getting into the room where she would be cut open and toyed with for hours, they moved her to another bed, and an oxygen mask appeared over her face. She was crying and snotty and a mess, wondering if this is what they saw every day. She apologized for her behavior and did not hear the response. Amid the sounds of her own sobbing, she heard them tell her to count backwards from ten.

Mom and dad . . .

Waking up was a process over a couple of days.

First memory: at some point she reached down to see how much she had grown, her hand seemed to hit at the top of her hip bone, when before it was a bit lower.

Second memory: every time her eyes open, someone comes in and stabs her leg with a giant needle and puts medicine in her veins. How can she stay awake long enough to ask anything or understand any of this?

At some point they said she was not paralyzed, that it had gone well, and she would not have to wear a brace on her body. This was great news, and she slept a hard, narcotic sleep that stopped the pain or any other feelings from showing themselves.

The car ride home was excruciatingly painful, and pain was not something she was very familiar with. It was scary, and it felt like her body was going to break. It felt too much for anyone to bear.

Home was not much better because on top of the pain that was now much stronger without the leg shots and IV drugs, she felt the guilt already. Her mother had to take care of her all day and all night. Her mother slept by the bed, but not on the bed so she would not hurt her at night. Sometimes she would hear her mom getting actual sleep and try to put off asking for medicine or food or water or help just moving side to side just so her mother could rest. She did not deserve to have her mother take care of her like this, all the time.

She did not think her mother deserved the burden of

watching the pain and suffering and having to take care of her. She felt awful for her mother's lack of sleep and constant nursing. This is another thing she was not told beforehand, that she would be a paralyzed zombie for months, needing help with everything, even scratching an itch. She was a burden.

She lay there, feeling paralyzed, feeling stuck in her own body. It was much like being in a nightmare she could not wake from, stuck inside and unable to respond. The pain was nauseating, constant, and the medication would wear off long before it was time for the next dose. Trapped in her own body, guilty for her mom's loss of time and a healthy daughter, exhausted, defeated, depressed, and traumatized—she tried her best to heal as quickly as possible so life could go back to normal for everyone. When it hurt, she made herself try to turn over. At times, it was useless, but every now and then, she felt some strength returning to her new body. This body felt plastic, stretched, and stiff—a mannequin with human thoughts and emotions.

The summer of lying in front of the TV, healing and taking it easy, was replaced with nightmares and constant pain. She fought it daily and tried to heal. Showering was hard, getting up by having her mother turn her to one side, hold her there while putting her into some stiff, seated position. Then standing up with her mom's help and walking slowly and painfully to sit in a chair in the shower and cry through the whole thing. Then the walk back to the bed and reverse the process. Sit down like a mummy and slowly lie down and back to the same position for months.

When she did finally get up on her own, she forced herself to do it through the pain and made it happen. It was enough. Everyone had to take care of her, especially her mom, and she just wanted her life back to normal.

Walking was ridiculous. Mummified teenager coming down the hallway into the kitchen to everyone's shock. They were happy for her movement. She knew it was probably too soon, but it was too long to wait.

The nightmares of being stuck inside her body would continue on and off for years, and it would take almost the whole year to really heal to the point of feeling somewhat normal. Still stiff and unsure, she went to dance class because the doctor said she could after a year. It wasn't a thought whether or not she was ready. It was just time. Time to be normal, time to try to be normal again. Little did she know that ship had sailed. For a few years, she would feel okay, but also feel the slow breakdown of her body.

Paralysis by surgery was not the outcome, but a different sort of paralysis took over slowly—stuck in her own rigid body for months after surgery, and then in her dreams, she was often stuck in that same body. The pain worsened over time, and over the years her body would fail her time and time again, with damaged discs and destroyed nerves showing up to physically bind her again.

A year they said. It would take a year to heal. But the damage was done.

Through high school, the nightmares and anxiety continued. Always the same, stuck in her body, paralyzed and in fear. The budding of what would become full-blown anxiety.

They take your body, and then your body takes your mind.

14

I spoke to Xander on the phone, and he told me he was going to get me out and not to go to treatment because they would keep me there for months. He spoke to my parents, and they told him their ideas about treatment. He warned me not to fall for it, and he said that he would get me out. I believed him because I had to. My bail hearing was emotional. My parents were there in the courtroom while I was shackled and cuffed in my orange jail clothes. I cried the whole time and don't remember much of what was said. I know my bail was high since I was a flight risk.

The sixth day into my jail visit, Xander told me he was going to pick me up that day. I was so excited I wanted to burst. His dad gave him the money to bail me out, which I had to pay back. Our plan was to return to J's apartment and figure out how we would get back to Texas. The court was aware that I would be going back to Texas. I had a "life" there. The car we came to Louisiana in was now in the custody of my parents. When they picked it up, they gave Xander his things that were in it.

A guard called me out of my cell for bail, and it took minutes to be back in my own smoke-smelling clothes, walking toward Xander. I felt great when I saw him. I hugged and kissed him. He had saved me from hell, and he was the only person who would do it. I had no intention of speaking to my parents now. I had given up on them entirely. I slept on a sofa bed that night with him, and I felt safe and thankful to have the jail experience behind me.

The next morning, we got a call requesting my presence

in court for a possible plea bargain. I went, and so did my parents. We sat with lawyers and a judge, and they went over my charges. I was not charged with the credit card theft like I thought, but I was charged with stealing from the hillbilly boss I worked for over a year ago. I felt like the situation was hopeless, and even though they dropped the cocaine charge, I was still facing a felony. The lawyer said that I need to sign this agreement to pay back the money the company lost and be placed on probation for three years. If I did not agree to that, I was facing four years in prison for forgery, and it would not look too great to a jury that I fled with my parents' credit card and was on the run for a year.

I had no one to help me and to tell me my rights, and I was scared and felt pressured to take this deal. I didn't want to go back to jail. I would not live through that much time. If I went back to jail, my life would end. If I took the plea deal, I could try to change my life. Did it matter if I did or did not commit the crime?

15

I look at her looking at me, and I know she can see right through the bullshit, right through to who I am. She wants to help.

But that moment passes quickly as she decides it's too risky. She is a judge, after all.

I want to cry out to her, "Please help! I am just a lost child who needs some guidance, not jail or drug treatment. Therapy, help, something!" I assume no one believes me or listens to me at this point. They think they know what I have done and assume I have done it for dumb reasons and I will go to jail.

I have felt pretty low in my young life—broke and on the road. There were times I thought we would die. It was hard to figure out where we were going to live or how. I wanted an adventure, but it was quickly turning me into just an eighteen-year-old runaway. In everyone's eyes, I was a fuck up—a young, selfish fuck up.

"*Maybe they were right,*" I later thought. I may deserve this. I signed whatever they put in front of me. They never offered a lawyer to me, and I don't think they ever intended to press actual charges, but they needed to find a way to bring me home and make me literally pay. This agreement took place outside of the courtroom, and it seemed a bit different than I expected.

Another path this whole adventure put me on: one of the conditions of my probation was that I had to live in Louisiana.

Well, that's fucking beautiful! They were hauling me right back to the place I ran from, just to watch me and punish me a bit more. So, I chose to move to New Orleans as it's in the state and so it fit the criteria. I had to work as a bartender as much as possible to pay rent, bills, and the back pay for my offense. It would take two years to pay off, and I don't know how I paid all those bills myself on the money I made. I had just started bartending so I was working at a place with great people, but not great money.

I lived with Xander, but he would not work. Again. This bothered me for a long time. Finally, a while into living there, I just could not understand how he could not even try to help me pay all this money back for our little adventure, how he could not help me with the bills and the rent. I gave him many chances. Finally, it was eventually time to end our relationship . . . It ended ugly with resentment and anger, but I knew at that point I had to get away for myself and try to be on my own.

Of course, within a few months of us breaking up, he got a job—bartending. I mean, really, I was doing that for years! He just went and got the same job as I had been doing and stopped talking to me for a very long time.

So I lived alone after that, always unsure about my future and questioning my past.

16

Isolation was a feeling I carried with me for most of my youth and into my independent life. I didn't ask myself if the things I said and did were coming from me. I knew they came from the part of me that wanted to please.

My friends, at an early age, were often hard to relate to. They were not interested in art or books. I wrote poems and stories as long as I could remember and couldn't find my people to connect with in my small town.

Part of my rebellion, though it was way out of hand before I realized, came from this isolation. I really believed that if I just got away and traveled, I could make friends and start over. This is not impossible or even crazy. It's just the way I went about it that was a bit crazy. In my naive brain, I thought I had to run away and leave the past completely behind. It was in my mind that to escape from what I disliked, I needed to cut all ties. That was hard, so in order to do it, I had to create another version of me. This version did not give a shit, just wanted to get away and stay away. I thought that I could do it.

I thought I wanted to do it.

I just didn't realize that to move forward you don't have to throw away your past. One foot in the past and one in the future. You are the sum of your past experiences, and that's that. So I felt the isolation for many years and often still feel it as an adult. Now I know I don't have to pretend to be you—I can be me. Not everyone will like me, but I will like me much better.

I can look back and see how the situation of running away as a young person looked so bizarre to my family. But I felt crazy living the way I did.

HELLO I'LL BE STEALING FROM YOU TODAY

I would learn many hard lessons, and I would lose myself. But later in life I would know better—who I am and who I am not.

I will always feel isolated because we all are. We are all just versions of something we can never really explain. No one will really know us. All we can hope is that we will know ourselves.

I enjoyed some of the moments in my new life, new friends and different people to talk to about real subjects I found interesting. Culture, food, friends, and a new start. I felt better for a while, but I still dealt with the nagging anxiety that was always there, waiting to come back and take over.

Fear was the constant, and it was becoming worse. I had made it through some really difficult shit, some drugs, and getting fucked up. Then I was a fucking fugitive. Now I was trying to just have a normal life, and all I could do was feel afraid, anxious, and never sure of anything.

17

You can run but eventually life catches up with you, and you have to face all the people and situations you ran from initially. This part is the worst because no one will look at you the same if you lied to them. You wonder what it was all for and are often left without many answers.

The payback for all the hurt you put out comes back slowly miserably painful. A big circle just to end up where you started. You break down and cry, finally trying to explain it all, but no one wants to hear it.

They thought you were nuts or dead. Or both.

They thought all the things you will never truly understand and you went through things they will never know, can't ever really know.

Everyone is confused. Some young girls don't make it back, and now you know why. The crazy shit you have been put through in this town and on the run, all of it hurt you in a deep, dark way.

You will never be the same person. Life is dirty and gritty, and you learned this, but at what cost?

Some things you can't get back. Losing parts of your innocence to the world, much larger than you ever imagined. It takes your eagerness, wonder, and drive to try new things, for a while at least, and you just say, "Fuck it. It's too hard. I'm too hard now." This place has made me feel anger, loss, hunger, fear, death . . . and then I realized it was all for escape. Sure, I was bored and so out of place. But that seemed to be true everywhere I went. I was out of place, just being me.

Anxiety Girl finally realized she can't run from Anxiety Girl.

nola girl

1

Southern Louisiana is full of things you may not find in other places. Some of these may be partly to blame for my confused youth. As a teenager hating the south, maybe I just saw the worst. Some are just odd. Some are not only here but seem to be more prevalent here. As a general rule, if you are different in any way from someone, they most likely don't like you even though they may pretend to when you're around. Your race, sexual orientation, religion, even your last name can cause you to be an outsider. It's that fucked-up Southern hospitality shit someone must have put in a brochure to lure visitors to the South.

And alcohol. It's everywhere. Parents tell kids not to drink while unwinding with a drink. Celebrations seem to be always centered on alcohol.

Drive-thru daiquiri shops selling cocktails and frozen drinks for those long drives. Drinking and driving . . . I mean, come on! Even I knew that was not fucking normal when I was sixteen and taking alcohol from my best friend's dad's daiquiri shop!

Family values here confuse me. Everyone has this family-first mentality where they look out for each other only. You better be related to, or know someone who knows someone, if you want a job or anything.

Yet these same people treat most family like disposable property. They don't appreciate, don't show love, treat aging parents like free babysitters, even having grandparents partially raising their kids, talk down to those closest to them, including family and especially children. They often hit kids.

HELLO I'LL BE STEALING FROM YOU TODAY

Generally they don't explain anything to their children or teach them anything. They are anger balls, swearing to Jesus to honor their family on Sunday, yet forgetting as soon as they walk out of church.

Sex education, or the lack of it. There seems to be no one talking about sex until it's too late. I don't know if this is some old stigma passed down from older generations.

Fake smiles all around. I was aware of this for a long time, but travel made me realize how much better it is to just lose the fake face and be you. It's okay. We don't all have to match.

No one is ever wrong, so don't try to bring that up. Nope. You must be mistaken.

Racist people! It's racism without a clue. Oh, and most of you are descendants of slaves or slave owners who had sex with slaves. So none of you who are from here are white. They are mostly mixed races, but if you are light-skinned enough to be considered white, you are racist for no apparent reason. Everyone is the same, acts the same. I heard a conversation where a "white" lady complained of being in court all day with mostly "niggers" . . . wait, so you are saying the black people who were in court for the same reasons you were there are somehow less than you, bothering you?

Bad drivers in stupid trucks. Ninety percent of the time the asshole is in a truck. Anger!

Food. It's usually drowning in butter. So it will taste good, it's filled with yummy artery-clogging butter. Most Southern dishes are filled with fat—most of the Southern people are fat.

Litter. It's all around the sides of roads and highways. It's like everyone thinks there is someone else to pick up after them.

Trailer houses. Shouldn't these be places to stay while you

build the actual home or work on a movie set or vacation? They have wheels. Homes have a foundation. Okay?

Yelling, talking loudly about your life in a public place, you know, the personal, private details that shouldn't be talked about in front of everyone. This is incredibly fucking stupid and tasteless. Have some illusion of decency and respect for those around you.

Marriages . . . most so fucking awful being divorced would be a vacation.

Arguing. See above. Couples, and people in general, talk to each other like shit for no reason.

Negative attitudes, shitty faces, killing animals for fun, dogs on leashes who never get love, nothing spiritual. No soul.

People never leave. If you go back to the same small town decade after decade, you will find the same people along with the new people they created who will most likely never leave either, claiming to love their home, family, and life. Seems to me that they just don't see a way out. That's why at a young age I had to get out, I needed to get out. I knew things were different in other places. I found many differences, some good, some awful.

It's not all bad here. This is just a look at what I saw often and I know most people growing up in the South see every day. You can get out, you can be different, you can shake shit up. It's okay to question these things and want more.

"You think you are better than us," is one of the craziest things I have ever heard and still hear used today. No one thinks that! You feel lower, so you project. We are all the same and can get what we want. You just have to go after whatever that is and not care as much about other people's opinions. They won't help you live your life, especially when it's hard. If you get some money or power, they may want something, but that's the only time they will be there.

Though I was young, rebellious, and unsure exactly why, maybe some part of me understood the depth of the negativity in parts of Southern Louisiana. I came back as an older, more settled-down person with a kind heart who likes people, and I am glad I came back as an adult because I see it all over again through older eyes. Many people I thought were close to me, that I grew up with, are complete strangers when I look at everything. I realize that maybe I was escaping something more than boredom, depression, all that. I did it the wrong way. I would never have hurt my parents if I could change that part. But, things are what they are and I can't go back. And I need to live in a much more peaceful and kind atmosphere. It's not running away. It's running to a much better place.

2

It's running to New Orleans.

New Orleans, oddly one of the cities with the highest murder rate, also has some of the real Southerners—people who will look out for you just because you live nearby or they saw you at the grocery store. They say hello, ask you how you are, and they really want to know.

At this part in life, rebellion was not necessary. I was on my own living my own life. But I think rebellion was just in me, a part of me, so I just said, "I need something to rebel against, so whatcha got?"

Luckily I found my people around this same time. They were all pretty aimless, even those of us who were in college or had jobs or both.

How we came to be friends is a mystery. A gang of misfits, all turning up at the same places at the same times, each in their own little circles. One from this group knew a girl from that group, so they started talking to each other now and then. Some of the girls dated the guys, who are friends, and they all became friends, and so on. The crew grew to be a regular group of fucked-up young people.

We were the "fuck it" group—eager to party, feeling superior to others for no particular reason, rarely letting new people in. You don't like it? It's probably because you suck. So we all became a little mismatched group of former loners who were artsy and smart enough to know we could pull off our little act. We could go out and run this town, be known wherever we went and always do whatever the fuck we pleased. That usually included alcohol and cocaine all night, and maybe some pills.

When you have all that access to alcohol and bars that never close and you have money and drugs are all around, it's hard not to get sucked into the lifestyle. It's not like we were lowlifes. Some of us worked in politics or had family members very high up in the land of Southern politics.

We had:

> a politician's daughter
>
> a preacher's son
>
> the offspring of most of the top-ranking officials at City Hall
>
> multi-generation-old-money, uptown-street-named-after-your-great-grandfather types
>
> celebrity assistants
>
> celeb lovers who are on the DL
>
> limo drivers who had more money than those they drove around
>
> some who had nothing but a lot of heart, and that's everything.
>
> a few whose parents had died and life had kicked their asses, yet they were strong and resilient
>
> a granddaughter of a world-famous madam
>
> a stripper or two
>
> oil money . . . lots of oil money
>
> some who had no money at all, the ones who offer to buy drinks for everyone or give you anything you need.

We went to these city hall parties and did the same drugs we did out in our dive bar with the people who ran the city! It seemed like no big deal, like having a drink. It just kept you up so you could get through your night. The inner circle partied almost nightly and on all major holidays.

Decatur Street was our red carpet, and we walked it regularly. The next members in our circle came out once or twice a week, and there were about ten in that group. Then a few, four or five who came out rarely, meaning once or twice a month. These few were also often spotted out alone, not letting anyone know they were going out on that night. They had another circle they were with from time to time.

The guys were mostly asshole skateboarders with attitude for no particular reason. Some of these guys were scary at times, drinking too much and getting physical, hitting ex-girlfriends. Most were losers, loose-cannon types who were not the types of guys we would have stayed around long except we all became oddly, incredibly close. Our guys weren't respectful, were rarely very easy to be around, but at the time it worked. Few were in college, some worked, some were the trust fund babies. They stayed the same most of the time while we seemed to add some girls to the group.

The girls were more of a mixed bag. Some from the South, some from up north who came and fell in love with the South. Most of us were in college and many of us had jobs and money—family money, old Southern money. The kind that you don't really speak of much, but it's there to catch you when you fall. We worked part time, too, mostly as bartenders around the city, and mainly for free drinks for ourselves and our friends. Girls can get bar jobs much easier than guys, and our guys were lazy anyhow and didn't do much. We didn't care at the time. It worked for us, and it was fun. Too much fun.

When we were the kings and queens of the bars of Decatur Street and a few others, there were times when we would go out that the guys would ride their skateboards through the

HELLO I'LL BE STEALING FROM YOU TODAY

CBD (Central Business District) and into downtown, stopping occasionally at bars for a drink or to flirt with some Betties along the way. By the time we met with them we were all pretty buzzed and ready to start the night of wide eyes and fast talking . . .

When I was a young girl I wanted to be a princess, a ballerina when I grew up. Later in life I wanted to be a goddess like Mia. I haven't introduced her yet . . .

But I sometimes wondered and even wanted to attempt this experimental art production I thought of. I tried to get a group of girls together and film it for a class final, but it never happened. Take what the skaters were doing, but get a group of ballerinas. We would wear full stage makeup, tutus, and pointe shoes or ballet slippers. We would twirl and jump through the city, stopping at bars to drink.

We would leave suddenly, attempt a tour jete or some double pirouette, maybe fall and get hurt. Then back to ballerinas through the streets! We would end at our dive bar, park our pointe shoes under the foot railing, and start getting fucked up, talking about our "run" through the city. We would even have one person with the video camera looking up from below as we land the perfect fouetté or grand jete right on the rough sidewalk of the city streets. We could have had the blooper reel too.

But this would be crazy, I know. People don't think of ballet as a street sport, one you could literally take on the road. Oh but what fun it would be. Traveling cocaine ballerinas!

3

Nola girls . . . nights out dancing to brass bands or old-school hip hop, sweating, laughing and having fun. Or daytime drinking on porches with friends, being free to be whatever you wanted to be. Living in New Orleans was the first time I got a real taste of that. No matter who you were or what you were into, you could find your people. The judgment was gone. Nobody cares what you do right or wrong, they only care if you are good or bad. And they can tell the difference.

Taking things too far is easy there, but you can pull yourself out too. Some do. For all the bullshit partying, there were so many great times.

Conversations with my friends about life, guys, sex, taking a shit in a public restroom, live music, food, bike riding, the fly, potholes, parking tickets, rent, uptown, downtown, Marigny, streetcar, stinky tap water, how hot it might get, stupid winter, bartending, waiting tables, art, college, tourists and their odd ways. We might meet up with a hot booty call late at night. Sometimes he might get more than one of us at a time, but he will not get a phone call the next day.

It was fun and like nothing else. It's different there. Culture is not going anywhere. It's in everything. I found out more about my own history and background living in New Orleans from my gay historian fellow bartender than I ever knew growing up. My Creole identity was revealed—the crazy Opelousas history.

Then there was bartending, busy nights in the Pontchartrain hotel bar, and the little restaurant down the avenue that was my first bar job, which I quit and went back to seven times in about nine years. That three-block area was fun, busy nights making money, pouring drinks while singing along to the live music. The choreography of bartenders is a flow I understood well. I was fast and could remember all of the drinks people ordered. Apart from being hard on my back, it was great. I met people at these places who helped me find myself. They were like family. They looked out for me and really cared.

I was blessed with an eclectic mix of people in the South, and my group of friends was also blessed with a strong bond. We have lasted years through the bullshit. Many of us are going to forever be family.

Life begins when you find where you belong. For me, that did not happen until I was out of my hometown, out of my comfort zone, and thrown into a world I knew nothing about. I found my way. Found myself.

4

We knew the right people, and all of the groups were keeping themselves going the same way, snorting cocaine. Some more than others. There was an accessible amount of drugs, and if you were at a Mardi Gras ball, government Christmas party, dive bar, or celeb dinner party . . . someone was always doing it. It was a perfect storm.

We were in our twenties on our own, and we thought this was pretty fucking ideal. At some point, we eventually asked, "Where does this end?" That was a question no one wanted to really face.

I can speak for myself: it started slow and grew fast. Speed felt really good to me and my BFF, and we were a dangerous combo. When I was on cocaine, walking down our block of bars felt like walking a runway. I felt secure, happy, and interesting to all the people I spoke to. I am sure to an outsider, we just all looked like a bunch of bug-eyed fuck ups talking too much and acting privileged. But to me, it felt free.

The truth of that time was that we mostly had fun. We were living our lives in a manner strictly forbidden by any normal social standards. Our attitudes were such that getting caught with the drugs was not on the horizon for us. We knew people, we worked for many of these people running this city. It was okay, on some level. We did our drugs openly some nights, right off the bar while we sat, talked, and drank. We never talked quietly about being fucked up—we were brazen. All of the factors that made us friends also made it a bit dangerous to be friends. We could get away with too much—had access to too much.

HELLO I'LL BE STEALING FROM YOU TODAY

In a city where you can drink alcohol all day and night if you please, it's only natural that uppers followed, I suppose. We also had so much more of a group mentality on cocaine. When we drank, the alcohol affected everyone differently, so some were super happy, some angry and scary, some quiet. But the cocaine put us all a bit more on the same level. We could talk all night, drink all night . . . we were just all happy to be super high in our own Studio 54!

The nights out dancing with the girls really stand out, there was freedom for me. We snorted cocaine and drank. We danced until we sweated all of that out, then did it again. Laughing, talking, hugging, we were truly having fun.

Cocaine can be like a therapy session, a fun one that you usually never want to end. You open up and really talk to your friends. It's like a love fest at best and a shit storm at worst.

The cocaine karaoke nights were pretty fucking hilarious. We were wide eyed, in a bar out of our normal area, another ward. We were marking our territory here. We sang so many awful songs and did not hold back a fucking inch. We yelled, sang love songs with death metal voices, had group performances partly choreographed. Right before we were to hit the stage, we would pile up five or six of us into a small bathroom stall, snorting key bumps and talking, ready for our silly performance.

Once the use of the drug became beyond social, our fun nights were a bit more anxious and odd—we tried to keep it together. Our brains can only take so much of this drug before they say, "ENOUGH, I NEED AIR!" We were heading for a breakdown.

5

I'm in my living room telling this random girl and my best friend about how much more convenient it is to buy cocaine before you go out—for many reasons, including not having to troll around looking for it, getting high earlier and maybe to bed earlier too, and the "Great Shitter Search," that sudden need for a private toilet, somewhat clean, in a very busy and very dirty city. The random girl is very offended by the subject, even though we all know once you hear the cocaine being cut or even smell it, it's poop time! And we all have experienced how it's just not easy to find a place to do such things while out at bars, crowded bars, dirty bars, whatever the case may be.

I am talking about taking a shit with someone I hardly know, and that's okay to me in some fucked up way because she is at my house while her boyfriend is buying drugs in the back room. She looks vaguely familiar even though my best friend says I never remember anyone, so who knows. Maybe I know her. Either way, here she is. Offended.

The rest of the conversation we had about cocaine including all nighters, strip clubs, nosebleeds—all okay. But talking about taking a shit, something we all do on drugs or not, has troubled her. I've gone too far. Ms. Sensitivity here can't handle this. That's just fucking stupid, so I decide to talk about shit even more.

I talk about all kinds of shit one might have after snorting massive amounts of drugs—thousand-baby-snakes shit, super-smelly-won't-stop-coming-out shit, can't-hold-the-shit-in shit, all-night shit . . .

My best friend and I are laughing so hard we are crying.

HELLO I'LL BE STEALING FROM YOU TODAY

She is trying to hold it together with her delicate little ass. This was too much for her sensitive personality.

At one point I realize I don't know her, so she can wait outside for her stupid boyfriend. I kick her out right after I give her a huge line of cocaine. I know she needs to poop as she is forced to wait outside.

What a hilarious start to my evening, little lady!

6

I woke up exhausted, Drained from my way of life. I'm not auditioning—I'm in school and work at a bar. I go to bars. *"Is this fun?"* I wonder. What parts are fun? Being out of my mind and body are the only fun parts. The rest is quickly downhill.

That year, the "sneaux" snow days, being snowed in by the deluge of white powdery bliss, the build up from socializing, the casual drug use and then the drugs before liquor, the skipping going out all together and just getting high . . . they progressed so fast that it almost seemed seamless. It was okay when we were in it. It was only when it became the main focus, the problems—the nosebleeds, the feelings of completely being out of control—then I knew I had enough and I needed to stop.

I'd sit there and think, *"You want to know more about yourself? Take a look at your friends."* Fucked . . . I'm fucked.

Then it's after midnight, and I'm walking around again having a lovely time, in love with all my friends again, feeling like we are superior. To what or whom? Doesn't matter. The feeling, that makes it true. The night is slow, nice, snorting cocaine leisurely while sipping cocktails and mingling around our little stage. Nothing crazy, and it feels good. Maybe my thoughts during the daylight hours are just my "sad me side," and this is the real me. I talk to some people who work in the film industry about getting some work. I get a call from a new agent that evening. Maybe this is just fucking life. People live normally during the day, drink a few at night, occasionally go out of their minds. Then it's back to business as usual. Who knows? None of my friends seem to care.

It's not a big deal creatively speaking. We are doing better in our classes. I wrote two plays high on coke, in record time! We are not doing it all of the time, we can stop anytime we want. Just not yet!

7

The thing about drugs is that it hardly ever stays that way, easy and fun. It does not plateau. It grows into another entity, a monster you befriended and let into your life. After a few months of it being fun and a bit crazy, it started to grow into us going out just to do drugs. No longer did we use the drugs to stay up and drink or make the party last longer—now the drugs were the party. We bought huge amounts of cocaine and were convinced we had to snort it all before the end of the night. There were no leftovers. No such thing.

Partying in bars, mixing and mingling with interesting people, and playing fabulous was no longer the goal. It now turned into another world.

One early morning after a particularly long cocaine-fueled night, we were going to make PB&J sandwiches for all the homeless people in our walking distance, quite a few. We'd bring them a sandwich and ask them about themselves while filming it. We thought it would make a great final project, and we weren't going to eat the food anyway. Seemed like a great idea until the shit wore off and we went into the rabbit hole, not yet able to sleep but unable to function and praying for sleep.

The night I really, truly realized this was becoming an issue was one New Year's Eve. We were out at our local bar, and it was incredibly crowded. Everyone goes downtown for New Year's Eve, the amateurs and the party monsters. The bar was standing room only, so we would go in for drinks and go right back to the Range Rover. We sat there and snorted drugs, drinking our cocktails and talking. Right before midnight, we all went into the bar and got drinks, but instead of heading to the river to see the fireworks, we headed right to the Range Rover to sit and snort. It occurred to me that night that we were taking it too far. It was becoming our life, and we could not go out without doing it, ever.

This went on for a while as well. I continued to try to contain it for myself, try to stop myself, but it was too tempting once out at the bar. The night was inevitable, predictable in the worst way. We were all gone, just fuck ups now.

The Hollywood crowd came into town just as I was sure we needed to stop. I was working for an older gentleman author, doing a whole lot of hanging out at celebrity dinner parties and making a few very interesting phone calls to schedule his meetings. To say he was an interesting character is an understatement, but I'm getting ahead of myself again . . . I was also trying to audition, but I'm sure I was not looking my best for those auditions. It's hard to party your face off all night and try to hold it together for an audition. I booked a few commercials and worked a bit, but I am sure the lack of energy during the day made a difference in my performances. After partying all night, you feel drained of energy and drained of happiness.

You're all used up, it's a joke. I would always hate myself the next day and swear to change. A few nights later I would be trying to get home before the sun came up, leaving my best friend's house after drinking all night, with a numb face and enough cocaine in my system to kill a normal person. Still unsure how we made it out of some of these nights alive, we would snort until our noses could snort no more. Going to bed (Valium or some other downer was a must.), or else you could lay there for hours, waiting for sleep to come.

8

They call each other goddess, a tight little group of ladies who love one another completely and pure. They are best friends, family, and holders of each other's secrets. They all know who the real goddess of the group is, Mia, the most demure, petite, soft-spoken, and reclusive of them all. She calls the shots, decides when the gatherings will be and when the palace will remain silent. Her two best friends live at the home with her in separate quarters so separate they could be different homes. Mia runs this beautiful estate and has taken ownership of the place after the death of one of her longtime male friends, clients, participants. The very elite and powerful and mostly male visitors are allowed to come to the palace for parties and special events. These same people also pay for all of the needs of the household, and then some. The money to run such a huge home and host elaborate parties is all there, in the hands of Goddess M and her two loyal friends.

Many political events and famous musicians' birthday parties have been held here. One evening there can be a black tie charity event with noted political figures, another night may be a party so wild it could be held at the Playboy Mansion. It's all up to the goddesses, and they choose very carefully.

The private events are planned by M and her two companions. These are theatrical, choreographed, elaborate affairs with a small guest list and a huge budget. Themes are often dainty for the Goddesses—fairies, ballerinas, bunnies, or maybe kittens wearing only body paint. Those who attend know they are here for a show, and they know they will slowly become part of the show as well. Goddess M considers herself very non-sexual, craving very little contact from anyone in this manner. She likes to be alone, but is happy to have the goddesses and a few chosen male visitors there when she calls. She loves her goddesses, and they adore her. Her sexual energy is best expressed in these theater-style events, she craves the attention and the spotlight. The guests are there for other reasons, sexual appetites for being beaten, dominated, and taken over completely. The group of goddesses knows the participants well, their likes and dislikes, they are studied and understood while the planning is underway. There is always a build up, maybe a performance, dancing, singing, and sometimes burlesque-style strip teasing. It's a beautiful show, and based on the wishes of those in attendance, they may be slowly added to the show.

Some like a bit of public humiliation, which is always fun to start with. There are some who will be taken on the stage and stripped down and spanked or berated for amusement of others. A select few just enjoy watching all of it, not really participating. The rooms that connect the stage room are set up, ready for the participants to slowly peel away, taken by a goddess or two, to enjoy their type of particular sexual delights. Goddess M slips away after the performance and will walk around, watching each room for a while. These shows delight her, they make her feel as though she is expressing herself through the others in ways she cannot or would rather not show.

At times, behind the mask, she cries for all she cannot be. She has a soul that longs for freedom of the body, and a body that keeps her prisoner inside.

Her anger is easily set free on these nights. There are clients desiring a particularly rough punishment—whips usually, some like chains. She is the one to enter the room when it's time to give these men or women what they want. She wears her signature handmade dark-purple, fine-lace gloves, which most recognize. She takes out her anger, aggression, and all of her feelings of inadequacy here. There is a buildup for some. Others start to be beaten before they even hear her enter the room. She is not angry at these people. These are her friends and she loves them. They seek this and she seeks this. It works out well for all involved.

Once she has relieved herself of the buildup of rage, she slips away quietly, allowing the goddesses to end the evenings the way they see fit.

After these events she might stay tucked away in her large palace for days, weeks at times. She will sleep soundly, will write poetry, or paint beautiful pictures. She will smile again and will swim in the warm pool or the beach at the end of her pathway. She will meditate and feel loved, and her two friends will join her some evenings for wine and long late dinners, and they will talk and laugh. It's a delightful life she has found, one many will never understand.

The men and women who participate in the theater events, as well as the goddesses, will deposit their monthly dues into the bank to keep the house running. Some will send gifts to her home, and most will send a little extra money for the freedom to be there when they need to and the privacy the palace provides. Everyone involved is happy to play their role. The palace is a peaceful oasis with vivid beauty in every detail.

There are occasional bursts of outrageous pain and crazed sexual desire.

It just depends on which parts you see. Much like the world.

9

This is not healthy, this relationship we have found ourselves back in. We both know it, but I know it more than you do because I remember more than you do. You get the luxury of blacking out shit-faced drunk while I was just starting to buzz around like a little silly bee, and suddenly I am stuck babysitting you again, taking you home or staying out in the bar and trying to avoid eye contact with you because you look at me with disgust and anger. At times I see you talking with friends across the bar, acting all happy, and you see me looking at you and become so angry with your drunk hate face.

In this second-time-around relationship I constantly feel as though I'm fighting to keep us together. Then there are times you just pull away from me, block me out of your life for a week or two. We see each other out with friends and you don't say much. I feel so confused and always like I don't know what's next. I expect a break up, but you just go back to normal after the crazy shit, and I let you, so we are both fucked. I know we are not right together but something keeps us here, *back* here.

Our friends all tell me the same thing: LEAVE. *He won't change.* I try, but I think that we can work it out.

But even after almost two years apart, it's more of the same shit. Yes, Xander, it's my fault because of this, that, and the other thing. Yes, I hooked up with jailbird Jesus . . . you and I weren't together then! We had broken up. Anything else you want to blame me for? I'm also responsible for global warming, gas prices going through the roof, and your parents' lack of empathy? Yes, I love fucking with everyone just to have you point it out!

After almost two years apart, Xander and I were back together. Many of our issues from the past followed us into the new relationship. He was angry with me, furious, blaming me for the previous break up, in his eyes it was my fault because I hooked up with jailbird Jesus when he was released from jail. At that time Xander and I were not together anymore. We were breaking up; it was that time right after a breakup when one person maybe isn't sure if this is going to stick. So he hated me, blamed me for everything wrong between us. He took no responsibility. And I thought we could work through that.

You are so angry with me. The main problem is that you think that just because you don't remember it, it did not happen the way I tell you, and so it's my imagination or I am overreacting! I often drop it, hoping it will just go away. I tell you I can't take it. We go out for a few nights, things are okay . . . then suddenly there will be another night when it will happen again. For whatever reason, you turn on me—on everyone, but especially on me. Our friends can laugh at it, they don't care because they don't have to live with the beast. I cry myself to sleep, and I am going to leave.

Suddenly, around this time, our little group of friends decides it's time to bring cocaine back on the scene and start using a bit here and there just to keep ourselves up a bit longer, party more and have more fun. This is trouble for us because when you do cocaine, you don't turn into an evil asshole, so it's a beautiful night for me! I get to go out, get along with friends and you, and you go home and eventually go to sleep. Maybe we are onto something . . . Just a bump here and there of the little white powder, and all is well in our relationship. I like cocaine a bit too much. I am a social butterfly and can stay out all night on this shit. I really enjoy people and the conversations seem really interesting and we all seem really fucking fabulous!

10

If the older me could see the younger me at a cocktail party, say we were thirty and twenty years old . . . she would walk up and slap her!

No, she would hug her. She might do both.

But older me would say, "Listen, bitch, you have to trust your gut instinct on everything in life, trust it. And don't give in to guilt, your own or other people's. Guilt is a useless emotion that will eat away at your precious time on this earth."

If you have been with the same guy for three years off and on, and he still has no job and you pay all the bills, this is what it will be a few years from now. Why would it change? He is comfy, and you feel guilty. Now you feel bad about hurting people, bad about the way he was the only one who helped you out of jail. But he helped you get into jail too, and he was snorting the rest of the cocaine while you sat in lockup. He should have paid for at least half of all this debt. Stop feeling bad for everyone else and start looking for your happiness now!

You deserve to be happy. Why don't you see that?

When you are older and look back at your dreams, what you really want in life—acting, fame, etc.—it will not compare to your desire to be happy and whole, to know yourself and know what you really want. People around you love you and want the best for you. You want something more, and you can get it.

Young me would think that older me was just a hot drunk mess. But if she would hear anything it would be worth it.

HELLO I'LL BE STEALING FROM YOU TODAY

In life we can't go back, but we can start from where we are right now and find that thing that we know deep down we want for ourselves. Listen to that voice.

It's there for a reason.

11

Standing motionless in this dive bar, I feel I could cry, scream, laugh deliriously, but I choose scary silence. Around me everyone is doing things I don't care about—talking and drinking and laughing and dancing and smoking and just fucking existing happily somehow. What is this? Where do I fit? I could scream and yell my fucking head off . . . No one notices a thing but their own little circle. I am shrinking into myself again and these insane giants grow, feeding on this life of insane anxiety, doom and gloom. They will feed on me if I let them.

Enter my mental demons stage right.
It's not me, it's you.
It's not you, it's just those two.
It's not them, but it's more. That guy, that girl, that whore.
I need to fly away but my wings are not working.

Some other defect of mine I won't be able to mend.
But I cannot stay here any longer.
Inside this bar.
Inside my head.
Beside you.
You in my bed.
I need quiet and maybe padded walls.
Or just a home with friends, dinners, phone calls?
For now I stand alone, watching the people live a life I don't want to be in.
I don't think I ever made a choice, now or then.

12

I wake up, face stuck to the pillow. Drool, I think. It's really sticky though. Going into the bathroom, I look in the mirror and see my face and hair caked with thick, red blood, and I have to scrub to get it off. It looks like I've has been beaten with a baseball bat or run over by a car. After, I take a shower, carefully blowing my nose. Nothing. It almost looked like fake blood—it was so thick and matted to my hair. What happened last night? My face seemingly exploded . . .

Going back into the bedroom, I see the pillow and sheets. More blood. Murder scene blood. This is crazy. I rip all of it off to wash on the hottest setting possible multiple times. Then I just throw the bedding out and get new shit. It's too much. What if I had been on my back? Would I have died in my sleep, on NyQuil and Valium, bleeding into suffocation? I tell my closest friends, "No more. We have to stop. Please don't do it around me, I can't see it or I will do it."

Then, hotel room, a large baggie of cocaine, drinks, cigarettes, a few close friends, and a hooker hired to lay there naked so we can snort cocaine off her body while we talk too fast and drink too fast and live too fast.

Typical Wednesday night, right? It's scary that it's becoming so common. Not always hotel rooms or hookers—that was just for fun. But the bags are getting larger and we are getting smaller. Our hearts cannot keep up with this. It's bound to kill one of us soon. At this point, we had decided that it was much smarter to buy drugs in bulk and sell some and get our shit free. It wasn't to make money, just to get free shit and be the people with the giant bag of cocaine.

Waking up this morning, I think, *"Really? What took place last night to get us to the point where we decided to leave the bar and get a hotel room to get fucked up? From that point, when did we decide to get a stripper to join us? Did we ask her to let us snort cocaine off of her naked body or did that just happen organically? How much did we snort, drink, and how long was this night?"*

Mornings after speed binges are brutal. The fun and free spirits from the night before are replaced with zombies, depressed and feeling lower than ever. Each time it's a bit worse. It hurts to open your eyes and even more to move. Scarier still are the mornings when you wake up feeling okay, maybe ready to start again.

These were often road trip days! Taking our little show on the road, we held the CD case with the line of coke on it for the driver to snort on the interstate. We all had ours and lit cigs, turned up the music and drove usually to the nearest beach, which was a few hours away. Easy drive on early morning speed.

What is going on in our lives? We have become something I don't recognize. These things seem normal, funny, even great at the time. This is not great. This is fucking insanity masked as fun. Normal people don't do shit like this. It's hard to imagine getting into this situation.

Waking up back at home, in my bed, I am so glad I did not stay at that hotel room. There is no way I could wake up in this luxury suite to this debauchery. This shit, in the light of day, can make you question your sanity.

13

After experiencing waking up with my face covered in blood, and knowing that I feel awful the day after partying all night, you would think I would stop. I wanted to stop many times, tried to go out and drink while everyone else did it without a second thought.

Another thing I thought would change everything was my health diagnosis. I had known for a while that I was suffering, in pain, and I blamed myself. My doctor convinced me to have blood work done, which revealed that I had two different kinds of arthritis in my bones, especially in my lower back. I had another bone disease, which I ignored at that time. I couldn't face it all at once. I tried to treat the arthritis and knew snorting cocaine was not good for my fucking bones, but I went back out there and did the shit.

The sad part was that after months of the same thing with the same people in our insane dive bar, it started to become monotonous. I didn't look forward to anything, but I needed my friends. They were my family at the time.

The highs were high at one time, but now the lows were even lower.

Once it was decided we were going "out" that night, the first thing we made sure we had was one of our dealers ready to meet us. My boss at the art gallery, where I was the manager, was one of our dealers. His apartment smelled of cocaine from the very modern hallway we walked down to get the shit. He had little hills, white powdery hills of cocaine, on his kitchen island. He also had a stripper pole in his place, and the first time I was ever alone with him outside the office he asked me straight out, "Can I see your pussy?" I was pissed and thought I would never speak to this man again, but here we were, back at his apartment buying bags of cocaine. He would cut giant lines from the white hills at one time, enough in one line to keep us going all night. Now, that was the appetizer. He was crazy, grew to be a friend, though a very strange friend who might at times ask to see your pussy. He was at least fifteen years older than us, always sweating and always snorting. I at least had the strength to say no to the shit at work, but he did it all day. I was amazed how much he drank and snorted all day while selling art and coming off as a bit of a jackass to most people. He sold a lot of art and a lot of coke. He was usually our first stop.

Then we would get dressed as though we were going out, but go to my friend's house instead and sit around talking, drinking, snorting. There was a bar next door to her house, so it made the most sense to go there. Every now and then we would walk over to this random bar. We made it busy some nights. Drinking in the same apartment after a while gets old.

At times I thought one of us was just going to drop dead. Just like that because it was hard to believe our bodies could take this. I think I was the only one who saw all of this as a growing issue and felt we needed to stop or slow down. When I talked about it, no one else seemed too concerned. It was just fun to them. Fun?

Some nights I went home before the sun came up. One of my rules: never see the sun come up after partying, it's not pretty. Try to beat the sun home! I have to at least do that, or I have gone too far. Going out at night and coming home when other people are starting their day is a bit odd—too odd and too far. It feels great when it's happening, but when it's ending, the wall is made of stone and you are hitting it with your fucking face! I would talk to my friend the next day and find out they stayed up doing the same thing until 10 a.m. It was too much.

Knowing my health was an issue I needed to face, I felt like I was killing myself to escape what I saw as a life of pain. I also felt a pull to do better. But often that came and went pretty quickly.

14

Once time went by and I knew my family understood some of what I had done and forgave most of it, I felt like I knew what was next. I just needed to make sure they loved me again and knew I never meant to hurt them. My anxiety had gotten huge. I could not be around the general public for long without wanting to scream or just fucking punch someone. I still did not fit in much. I had a few people I felt good with, but that was hardly enough to call my day-to-day activity a life. It was time to go on to the next place.

When you get to the point in life where you don't see the point in living, it's hard to go on. I wanted to go on, but to what? For what? It looked bleak.

I wanted it to look like an accident, so my family would not feel let down again. It happens all the time, mixing the wrong pills with alcohol and just falling asleep. I never wanted to hurt them, this way they could just think it was out of my hands.

One of the harder decisions was how much of a trail of crazy, if any, should I leave? I need to clear the house of some signs of crazy, but not all. It can't be too perfect.

Then I started to wonder if I should leave more crazy behind, so that way people could think I was just too far gone and had gone "to a better place" as they like to say. Should I make plans for a day or two after I do it, dinner with a friend? New tattoo? Something to show I planned to have future plans? So many decisions and loose ends.

One scenario played in my mind often, mainly because I thought it would be a statement of some sort and make me

HELLO I'LL BE STEALING FROM YOU TODAY

partially famous. Take a gun and shoot myself in the vagina. Treat my body like the disgusting men had done before, and just shoot myself that way. You can't come back from that, I'm assuming, I haven't heard of anyone ever doing it. I was going to dress very-old-Hollywood style and film the whole thing—very dramatic. That's what I wanted. I hated guns though, and the constant guilt over hurting my family shut that idea down. I could never do this as long as I had family who loved me.

So, falling asleep eternally was really my only option. I had to go away low key, just move on to the next part of existence, whatever that may be. I wondered if it would be a partial let down and hoped I would not regret it, it being so final. After a certain number of mundane days, it was just time to make a solid plan.

I bought pills from a friend, a few at a time, saving them so no one would be able to say I bought all those pills the day before so then suddenly it's on purpose, blah blah. So, I just bought a few here and there . . . lived as much as I could, disgusted with most of the world, apologetic to the rest.

I put all my pills in my lucky box, and I waited.

Until I had enough pills, enough strength, and just enough of it all.

15

Little girl lost inside of me, afraid of the past afraid of who I could be.

Stuck in the shadow of my own regrets I hold the girl hostage, not sure if it's safe.

Safe to move forward into the future, into who I can become.

Knowing what you don't want to be does not help you to know who you are.

Not knowing is no reason not to try to move beyond this little girl.

Ashamed of the things she has done, afraid to live her way.

She got stuck in the middle, where she will stay.

Until the real me can come out and take her hand and says it's okay, live your life for you. The future is going to be different, you will be free.

Free from the girl you didn't want to be.

16

Working as an actress, I find it so freeing to be someone else. Glamour, Hollywood, luxury . . . the expectation I had and really believed in completely. It's so nice to know it's not insanity. I am an actress, born to be! Waking up at 4 a.m., driving or taking some white van to set, seeing the trailers (the good kind) on the film set. The preparation, the hair, makeup, costumes, even the waiting around. It's a buildup of pure bliss leading up to the work, and it's so sad when the work ends. It's what I was born to be. The whole Hollywood machine is beautiful to my eyes.

It seems like each time I make it into the right circles of people, get to audition for speaking roles in front on casting directors or onto the really serious sets, and get so close . . . something caves in. You can't fall off of the Earth in this business. You have to be working all of the time to get more work. But it's not Hollywood, it's Hollywood South, so jobs are harder to get. At times it's frustrating. No one who knows they are an actor is happy working as an extra for long, but you make contacts, so I do it.

At my highest point, I worked on a few commercials and had been a stand in for a few actresses of note. I auditioned for and been cast in a feature film, a speaking role, and I began to work as a personal assistant to a celebrity, a writer. It was coming together. There were dinner parties with famous celebrities, writers, and Hollywood types. We were able to attend private screenings of documentaries, and talk about Hollywood in general. There were meetings with producers, and I was getting great feedback on my acting style from the people I was around. I was learning from those who were working regularly in the business.

It felt like things were heading in the right direction. I spoke to quite a few very famous people weekly, at least.

But things have a way of fucking up in the most fucked-up ways. I don't anticipate that it will be the horrible circumstances, not me, who ends this ride.

17

When we heard that a hurricane was heading our way, at first none of us gave it a second thought.

There are many hurricanes, but they always go to the left or right of the city. This one was growing larger though and increasingly becoming a threat. It was just two days before the storm hit that most of us left the city. We took only what we would need for a day or two, still thinking there was no way anything was going to happen. Just maybe some flooding.

Hurricane Katrina destroyed everything. It took so many things from us, homes and belongings, all of those things we expected to find intact. But it also took so much more. It took our bike rides to breakfast, our favorite coffee shop, our neighborhood crackhead, our neighbors. Our day to day lives were just gone. No one could talk to each other, cell phones were not working for weeks. Katrina caused us to learn to text each other out of necessity, and we still do today. We could ask our friends "Are you okay?" and they could message us back. It's all we had. We were scattered and afraid, watching our city go underwater.

The party was officially over for us, for the group of toxic friends. Most of us had no idea what to do, where to live next. We questioned everything. We also stopped the drugs, just like that. If anyone was still using, I didn't notice. Most people seemed to be having a few drinks, passing out exhausted from this tragic shit.

There were horror stories of rescue workers tying dead bodies to trees in the aftermath so they would not float away. One of our friends saw a kitten screaming out for help and went over to save it. It seemed to be caught, so he was trying to get its paws free. He realized the kitten was stuck in the streetcar track and under the bloated body of a dead person, laying there left behind. This storm was a nightmare we could not wake up from.

Time goes on. The dead bodies get put into a warehouse in the CBD, the dead grass slowly got its color, and the refrigerators stacked as high and far as one could see were all picked up and disposed of. Slowly restaurants opened up, hoping locals would forget about the disgusting conditions in the aftermath of the storm, and bars never really closed. After a while, the streetcars came back, and some locals came back. I thought it felt very different there for many years. It felt scary and it reminded me of that fear the day we took a boat down our street and to our flooded home. I loathed it. But time has a way of allowing you to remember the good stuff and to let go of the hurt.

Going back was a mixed bag of feelings and fears. I didn't want to be a cokehead anymore. I wanted my friends to be normal people as well. As normal as my friends can be. I mean nothing crazy like 9 to 5 jobs and talking about retirement and 401K bullshit. Just to be better versions of the psychos.

But everyone had scattered. Moved away and moved on. Some came back, but they were different, all of them. It was as if the storm stopped the bullshit and made the group dissipate. We still see each other now and then. Though none of the couples are together anymore, some of the older friends still talk and raise their kids together.

Months later I would look back at the storm and get the feeling that something needed to happen to end what we were doing to ourselves, perhaps not a storm of this magnitude, but something needed to stop us. Katrina was what did it, and for most of us, we did not do drugs again. The hurricane ended the perfect storm.

18

Driving into New Orleans ten days after the hurricane hit, we knew we were going to have to sneak into the city. It was closed to anyone entering besides emergency teams, which were not really interested in coming in. My dad, my boyfriend, and I went to see what the fuck was going on in our apartment. Was it underwater? I watched TV constantly for all the coverage I could find, but I never saw my street exactly. I would see different parts of uptown, blocks away from where I lived that were completely underwater, people walking with water up to their necks. Then I would see another video of the other direction, and it was dry.

I could not stand not knowing what was going on. I wanted to try to rescue my cat, and I just had to get back there.

We drove in on Jefferson Highway instead of I-10 to try to get into the city. Before we would get to the exit, we hit a huge patch of water under an overpass. It was deep, suddenly very deep. And we could smell the stench of death in the air. It was scary as fuck. We turned around and took I-10. We made it to our exit and came to the National Guard before getting to my neighborhood. They said we could not enter at that very point but hinted that the other streets were not all being guarded.

So we took the hint and drove a few blocks down and got over the tracks they were guarding and drove the few blocks to Carrollton Avenue, the street where we lived, though it was a main street and very long. We were still about twenty blocks from the house.

It was scary at this point. The city was quiet and stinky, and there was a feeling of fear in us for some reason we could not quite explain. It felt like someone, someplace, was watching and ready to shoot us at any point. We drove on, as far as we could—then the water came. It was all around us and the truck we were in was obviously not going to make it much further. My dad got out of the truck and saw a boat. I mean this boat was just sitting there, waiting for us—a tiny little row boat, ready for us to borrow. It was scary, but we got in.

Boating down the street we once drove daily and rode our bikes down and walked on was surreal. It felt scary, like we were targets, vulnerable and in the middle of black water. We still had about eight blocks to go. The water was getting deep fast, and the guys could not feel the bottom any longer. The sticks they used to row were now hitting cars. We saw the apartment, and it was great. Even though the water was very high, the house was also high from the ground. The place sat on a small incline, and the house was then raised with five huge steps leading to the front porch. The water was lapping at the porch, so the boat docked right at our door.

We went in knowing that most houses were broken into in the city—many of our windows were broken. It was a bit scary, dark inside the house during the day and smelling of storm. That is the name of the smell that cannot be named . . . storm smell. Even though my dad and my boyfriend both warned me that the cat may not be alive, she came to the door the minute we opened it. I cried and held her as they locked our metal front door. We went into the house and saw some water coming from the floors, and with a quick look, it did not look awful. Not as bad as other places we saw. The car sat on the side of the house, underwater. We grabbed the few things we could take on the rowboat and were about to leave.

Suddenly, noise. Boats, motors, and people were outside.

HELLO I'LL BE STEALING FROM YOU TODAY

I ran to the locked metal door to see some official looking men in huge boats strapped with guns driving down our street. There was quite a few of them, and they made waves on our front porch. Our little boat was now about to float away . . .

Xander was in the bathroom, and he had the keys. I ran into the bathroom and said, "Keys now! The boat is floating away!" At first he didn't react, and I freaked out and said, "Give me the fucking keys to the door now!"

I made it to the door, found the key out of all the keys, and was determined to get this door open. Just before the boat started to float away, I opened the door, and my dad grabbed our boat, docking it higher on the porch.

It was time to go.

Heading back with the pet taxi and a bit of important documents and the stuff we could grab, we rowed back the opposite way. It felt even longer going back this way. It was scary and felt like we needed to get the fuck out of there.

We would not be back for months, and when we came back, the grass was gone—all of it was dead. The water was toxic and it had killed everything. The smell had taken over the city. It would enter your nose and not leave. I found it difficult to believe I could learn to live with this smell. The bugs were now everywhere—little gnats feeding on little unseen bits of death.

Walking through the apartment, we tried to decide if we stay and try to clean up or go. The kitchen was in the back, and once we got back there, the fridge was alive. It was making a noise, a buzzing alive noise. Things were in there and they were thriving! I called the landlord and told him we were trying, but this fridge needed to go. He suggested we clean it! That was it. After a few hours of trying to find something that would make it okay, we just knew that it wasn't okay anymore. This was not home, not a life, not meant to be lived in. It was death and sad and we had to go.

Sometime later, we would come back to get the things we could salvage, and that fridge still sat there, alive. We taped it shut, making sure no one would ever have to open it. We took less than half of the stuff that was in the house, only what we really thought was in good condition or we could clean. Later, we would throw out more stuff and have to start over with almost everything in our lives.

Where to go? That was the question we would ask ourselves for years to come . . .

19

Not only was my city destroyed in the storm, but my best friend in the movie business, the celebrity I worked as an assistant for, who really believed in me and wanted to help me get work on an upcoming film based on one of his books, was suddenly gone. He killed himself. There are not enough words to describe the pain of that loss, but I'll sure try soon enough.

Then, after these two large and very sad obstacles, I left the city and the entertainment industry.

I assumed I would be back after a few months . . .

But life changes you, and you get comfortable with a quieter life for a while. You think it's your fault you are not booking work, but how can you when you are no longer local?

I would get a few close calls, but . . . I slowly allowed it to become a dream I would release. The problem with that is simple. It's too hard to let go of something so meaningful to you. I can't simply not want what I absolutely know I want.

I have some regrets, like meeting these celebrities and not asking more questions. Not asking for help. One of the first film sets I ever worked on, as an extra, was a very big set. There were many people in this crowded cafe scene. I was just one of many, just having to walk over and over in front of the camera as the scene opened up. Dustin Hoffman approached me late in the thirteen-hour day. He told me, "You're a professional, I can tell. You will do great work."

This was a moment I never expected, so nice to hear. He spoke to no one else on set. I regretted not reaching out to him once filming wrapped, just saying something. But I felt frozen, just glad he spoke to me,, even grabbed my hand when walking by late in the day . . .

The last film I worked on, I got to walk the red carpet and meet my absolute favorite celebrity ever: Angelina Jolie. After meeting many famous people, only a few really stood out. Angie is that being to me, the one to work toward. I spoke to her on the carpet about Nola, the hurricane, the film, and this conversation lasted longer than I expected—it was a moment. I went to bed that night full, happy, and just wishing for one thing. I would have asked Angie, "Will you be my real friend?" Sounds dangerously stupid, and could be taken as a stalkerish thing to say, but I really meant it. "Can I learn from you, talk about acting and adoption and helping others, get to know someone who seems so much like me in this business?" It is still a regret that I did not just come out and ask to speak to her again. About anything.

Fame. People are mesmerized by it, talk about famous people with disdain while adoring them or feeling jealous. Some famous people complain about the issues that come along with it.

I would take that criticism, that ugly side of gossip and paparazzi without a second thought.

Because it's the process, the work, that is so beautiful.

Madonna said, "I traded fame for love, without a second thought."

>
> Words that always make sense.
> Maybe it's not too late.
> Some dreams never die.
> No matter where she goes it's there.
> As hard as you might try.
> Some things stay with you.
> There is a reason why.

20

Growing up is hard.

Being grown up is even harder. This will forever be true.

Not sure if I will ever really know who I am or grow into a woman, a grown-up type individual. I'm okay with that now, going with it rather than wondering why. Maybe it's better this way. I'm a perpetual girl in some ways, but a grown-up, too.

Some say I'm a late bloomer. What the fuck is that flower reference? If I'm a flower, I'm one of those that open up in the sunlight, seemingly bloom, then go back into myself in the dark of night. I'm a fluctuation flower.

After many experiences, insights, choices that were good and bad, memories made and lost, here I am. The next chapter of my life will always contain parts of my past, but moving forward is next into some sort of flow I can handle, happiness sought and negative people ignored. I thought I would have figured it all out by now. I thought everyone just did. I'm learning to seek out those I want in my life and find the experiences that help me grow. I once thought I owed something to those in my life, needed to be and do more. Now I see that I can just be me and the ones that are still around matter.

I matter.

hst girl

1

I have been here in Woody Creek for two days, and I already feel emotionally drained. I have been on a roller coaster of highs and lows, and the lows are just awful. I may be in over my head. I don't know if I was hired as a writing assistant, a maid, or some kind of sexual toy for an old man. Sometimes I feel as though I'm in the middle of something so huge, I can't even fathom it. I know this man is full of insight and is a genius in his own way. I listen to every word he says, and I enjoy when we are sitting and talking. I feel like I am at times immersed in art, watching something few have seen. Hunter is trying to write, and when he does this, all the stories that cloud his head are discussed at length, and I adore it.

But other times, I see a man who is in desperate need of reassurance, and my job becomes boosting his ego. To remind him of the words he has written in his past, I read to him from his own books. I read flattering quotes about him from other authors. I read articles written about him, talking about his huge effect on mainstream media. This helps remind him of the important work he has done and that he is a great writer. He no longer believes it. Hunter sees himself as his past, and the man he is now is not an acceptable reflection of what he remembers.

2

When I returned to New Orleans after living in NYC for about a year, before Katrina, hit, it gave me a whole new perspective about where I lived. Nola was easy. The whole South was easier. It was such a good feeling to go back to there and be able to get five or more errands done, have lunch with a friend, and still have energy to go out at night. In NYC, it could take all day just to run two errands because the city was so huge—taking the subway everywhere, walking, standing in lines. I would return to my one-room apartment exhausted and dirty. Even the undersides of my fingernails would be tainted with the filth of the city. Going out at night in NYC required careful planning, and the day after had to be pretty open because everyone would be walking everywhere and be hungover and sore the next day.

Maybe this is more specific to me because my body is always hurting and most days it's hard to move around. So, a night of drinking and sometimes doing cocaine in NYC would include walking all around the huge city, all before 2 a.m. Then, once we were done with the night, there would be the last long, dreadful walk home as the sun was rising. Yet, where was home? We often couldn't remember. We walked, taking directions from each other, from our scattered memories of finding the bar we ended up at, until we would finally catch a cab.

One night, I got into a cab with my boyfriend and gave the driver our address. He drove about four blocks, under an overpass, and then we were home. We were right down the street from our house, completely lost.

The point is this: in Nola, you can go out all night without walking miles. It was better. Always feeling rushed, crowded, and lost was not my idea of home. It was time to get far away from that place and back to the place I thought I was sick of living. I realized it was not the location, not the South, that had been the problem. It was me. Maybe I tried to run from some of my own issues, drugs, pain, anxiety. Maybe I felt my issues would stay in the South. But in NYC, I was still stuck with me and everything that came with it.

One night over a bottle of wine and a few hours of discussion, we had decided that we didn't like it here, so let's get out. The next day, we sold all of our stuff, gave some away, and packed up as much as we could fit into our little SUV. We left so fast. Within twenty-four hours of deciding to leave, we were packing. The next morning, bright and early, we left and didn't look back. We drove for two straight days, taking turns trying to sleep and driving like fucking maniacs. We'd really had enough of that city! In the two days of driving south, I figure that I most likely could have only gotten three errands done and maybe hit the grocery store in NYC.

Once I got back into Nola, I found an apartment in just a day—a real apartment, with rooms separated by doors. The apartment's living room was the size of the entire NYC apartment, only it was half the price. From there, I quickly got back into my life. I got my old job back. I had found bartending dreadfully boring before moving. Now, it was a charming job in a piano bar in an old hotel. I made real money and worked a lot less. It felt so much easier, and while I was gone, the celebrities had started coming to Nola more. The film industry was slowly moving to the South, and that was my dream for as long as I could remember. Having real films meant real jobs for actors here, I thought. So, I was ready for it. I worked on the set of as many films as possible as background characters and featured extras. I was cast in a

HELLO I'LL BE STEALING FROM YOU TODAY

regional commercial as the lead and did stand-in work. I had a lot of close-ups. "The camera loves you," they said to me. I loved it, too.

Walking into work one afternoon, late as usual, my gay best friend was working the bar while I got myself ready. I walked in, and there was an older man at the bar with his back to me, with the news channel blaring loud and the AC turned so high I immediately felt uncomfortable. I hit the thermometer to raise the temperature and walked out. I didn't see the man's face. I just went straight to the kitchen and started making my coffee. My friend came up to me and said, "Did you see who was at your bar?"

"Nope, I just turned off the AC and came in here."

"It's Hunter S. Thompson," he said, and I was surprised but figured that was one famous person I would most likely not end up talking to very much. I loved his writing and knew some of his life, though not much. I just knew *Fear and Loathing in Las Vegas* had recently come out, and I saw it and thought Johnny Depp had maybe played the character a bit crazier than the real-life man—perhaps he took his writing too literally and made a character out of the person. I thought Hunter would be pretty easy to handle, wouldn't want to talk. He was old, right?

Back in the bar, I got set up. I felt him staring at me, but I didn't know what I should do yet. Kevin, my friend, had just refilled his coffee and his cocktail, so I just continued setting up. He stared at me and read his paper, and I got a bit nervous. He didn't say anything, and neither did I for a while. It felt like forever, but was most likely about ten minutes. Finally I walked around the bar to do something on the other side, and he called me over.

He says, "Do you know who I am?" I hate when people ask that. It's an assumption that you must know them.

I say, "Yes, I think so."

He says, "Good. I want to know who you are." He is still holding my hand with both of his, having never let go of it from our handshake.

I say, "I'm Heather, your bartender."

He laughs like a madman and says, "This is going to be fun!" He holds my hand a moment longer, looking at me with a bit of crazy in his eyes. Releasing my hand, he says, "Stay close by."

Okay . . . I walk out and into the kitchen for some air. What is this guy's deal? And why is he making me feel out of place in my space? It's not the celebrity factor. I have met my share. It's him, something about him. He's just odd.

I return, and he has guests—two women. And he does not look happy about that. They start ordering food and drinks on his tab, and he is annoyed. He is drunk, but clearly they are not the drinking buddies he is looking for. After they drink and eat on his dime, they suggest going up to his suite. He agrees and asks me to come over. I walk around the bar, and he asks me to please get a bottle of Chivas whiskey from the hotel, hands me $100, and says, "Please bring it to my room with a real glass."

I say okay and close his tab out. By the time he signs his receipt, he has trouble standing. I'm not sure if it's the alcohol or pain he is obviously feeling, but he can't walk very well. One of the ladies produces a wheelchair she gets from the hotel and asks him to sit. He is pissed.

"Fuck you bitches. I don't need a fucking wheelchair! You dirty whores, what the fuck do you know? You're stealing from me, you whores!" He tries to walk a bit, but stumbles.

One of the ladies says, "Just ride. It's better, and no one is here. It's just an elevator ride." She seems to calm him a bit, and he sits.

HELLO I'LL BE STEALING FROM YOU TODAY

He looks at me and says, "See you soon, right?"

"Yep, I will be there."

Ringing him up for a bottle of Chivas at the hotel is a ridiculous amount of money. The hotel charges by the shot and is not going to discount alcohol. The bar is empty, so I walk a block down the street to a corner store instead. I go there often. He could buy three bottles at the store for the price of one at the hotel. I buy his alcohol and put the change in the bag. I walk back, peek into my quiet bar, and take the elevator up. I then walk into an odd scene.

Considering they only left the bar about twenty minutes ago, I can't explain why the women are wearing robes and seemingly nothing else. It's strange, and I have no idea what I'm walking into. Hunter looks happy though and is very impressed that I walked to a store to get the alcohol, so he gives me a $50 tip for the extra effort. *"Nice,"* I think, walking out as fast as possible.

But my night is just beginning. My bar telephone rings when I walk back into the bar, and it continues to ring most of my shift. Hunter has a direct line to me at the bar, and he has decided that he must speak to me about all the things that pop into his brain that night. It's a slow night at the bar, but I am now busy with his random requests.

Still thinking this would be just for the night, I enjoy it after a while. He is funny and seemingly harmless. I talk to him on the bar telephone about many subject—politics, film, women, the South. He calls me up to the room often to deliver room service, which is not my job, but he demands I am his only visitor to the suite. We talk for a while when I'm there, and by the time I get back behind the bar, the phone is usually ringing, I already know who it is.

3

Once I was HST's pet, that was it for me. My days were his, and he wanted a lot of my time. Since I was pretty bored with day-to-day life, I was glad to have a completely different person to talk to daily. Not only was he old enough to be my grandfather, but he was a famous writer with famous actor friends stopping by the hotel or calling the suite. He was interesting and found me very interesting.

This was off-putting at first. I assumed he was going to do that thing men do even though he could hardly walk—try to get me to strip for him or some other weird shit. But it wasn't like that with him, and we had so much to talk about that the days flew by. We shopped and, at times, I drove us places. We left the hotel to go to the movie set he was in town to visit and write about. We attended fancy dinner parties with wealthy New Orleans celebs and visited Hollywood. At one of these parties, we were given the chance to watch a never-before-seen documentary about 9/11 from a very well-known actor.

I had met famous people before, but these parties were intimate and at the homes of people I respected and wanted to learn from. I felt like it was the beginning of my dreams of acting becoming a reality. This industry is all about who you know, and he knew lots of important people. He told me that he wanted to help me, making me feel pretty great. I felt like I was accepted into his life quickly by most of his people. Some looked at me as though it was me who begged my way into his life, but had they known how we met, they may have felt differently.

HELLO I'LL BE STEALING FROM YOU TODAY

Hunter was quickly becoming a mentor to me, reading some of my writing and giving me feedback. I enjoyed his world, or what I saw of it in New Orleans. He was busy and interesting, and we got along and had fun.

However, there were days when I saw a glimpse of what he was really becoming—old, in pain, drunk, doing cocaine often, taking pain pills, and feeling angry at what he had become. Because of this, he would lash out at times. It was scary, and I was around for a few outbursts that made me want to run. Luckily, we were rarely alone, and never when we were alone did he act this way.

When he had an outburst, it felt like the room lost all control. Everyone seemed affected and felt the stress of his powerful personality, roaring with anger and demanding everyone respond immediately. I would usually end up in the car with his wife, Anita, who I adored. She seemed so fragile and nice, like a good person in a bad relationship that was once her ideal relationship. She was sinking though and had enough because most of his anger was directed at her, just as we all seem to hurt the ones we love. One night, we left a dinner party with him screaming about something I didn't understand at the time. We were in a mad rush to get him back to his room. He rode with the men and Anita, with me. I figured that this—dealing with his anger—was all part of my job, but I wanted to know more. I needed to know what was setting him off so quickly.

I said to Anita one day, "Please help me understand this because if I am with him and he breaks down, I can't help him." She gave me an example, and as I would learn later, this was a common anger trigger. At the last dinner party, Hunter, wheelchair-bound and pissed about it, had been asking to go to the bathroom. He asked Anita because he needed help standing, going, that sort of thing. Before he made it to the bathroom, he had an accident, something that happened more often now. He was angry and embarrassed. He felt like an old man and wanted to hide from the world.

I knew immediately how awful this must have been for a man who was once so filled with life and had been on the move at all times. He had chronic pain from a broken leg, a broken hip, a hip replacement, a back condition, and surgeries in the past, so at his age, it was done. He was not going to heal. He didn't have a slow or declining health—a chance to accept his conditions and learn to adjust to them. Everything happened so fast, and these injuries took away his ability to walk or live as he wished. They took his dignity.

I was sad for him and I wanted to help. I offered my friendship and tried to get him to write. According to Anita, that was my first priority in this job. Just get those words on that paper! We ended up talking most days and writing very little. He was so interested in my life, what it was like for me growing up in the South. The same life I loathed and ran from, he wanted to know more about. We talked endlessly about topics I once thought very boring, but he sparked in me a new interest in my own history.

He could be a bit angry when Anita came into the room, and often, they would argue. That's what most couples are like, I figured—it's hard. So I kept my distance and minded my own business about that. He told me she treated him like a sick, deranged old man or a dying child who was a burden. I heard versions of both of those statements a few times. I felt like I should not be there at moments, but he wanted me there as much as possible. At first, I paid little attention to what he was saying, just assumed it was couples' shit. But as the days went on, I saw some examples of this. I heard her talking down to him and, in so many words, calling him an embarrassment to her.

HELLO I'LL BE STEALING FROM YOU TODAY

For the time he was in Nola, he asked me to work with him and then, one day, asked me to come to Woody Creek upon his departure. I could handle working for him in the hotel I had worked at for years on and off. I knew this place well. I could sneak into the kitchen and make my Starbucks coffee or go down to the bar and have a quick drink with the staff that was covering for me. I could take a vacant room in the hotel and not tell him about it because he wanted me there, but I needed space. I felt this was smart. I could be nearby but sneak away to rest. I could also go home at night or whenever I needed to and sleep in my own bed. I was free, and I knew my surroundings. Going to Colorado seemed like another animal, one I was not sure was friendly. I told him I was going to think about going to his home, Owl Farm, but I would definitely be there at the hotel each day he needed me—which was every day.

I was happy not to be doing drugs, not to miss them. Even when those around me were snorting cocaine, I did not want it at all. I just wanted to have a drink now and then and enjoy this very odd experience.

We had an exciting few days coming up, going to a movie set and to a few dinner parties. I looked forward to all of it, and again I was staying at the hotel, ready to go whenever he called. One morning, when I was staying on the floor above his, he called my cell phone and said that I needed to get a private jet out of Nola for him that day. This sounded crazy, and I thought he was being silly, insane, or that he was just drunk. He liked to fuck with people, especially phoning them with random shit, so I wasn't sure what to think. This call was followed by a message from Anita requesting the same thing. I was to try to locate someone with access to a private jet that day.

I wasn't sure why suddenly his time here was over, and I

had questions. I was sad about it, but I started making calls. I had a few friends in high political standing and some very old-money friends. I called all of them. Before I could get word back from most, he had decided on first-class tickets out of town on a commercial plane, which he could get quickly and would take him out of town ASAP.

It all went by fast. I went to his room at the hotel, and he was sitting in his chair, looking sad, drinking, and smoking. People were packing, and it looked like they were almost done. I tried to talk to him. He asked me to just please come to his home. I wanted him to stay, but Anita seemed to want them gone immediately. They didn't want to wait for a private jet, which is why they had booked seats on a commercial flight, just thanked me for trying, and handed me some $100 bills. I had already been paid and said it was fine, not to worry, but Anita insisted I take the money.

I was confused by this. I talked to him a bit and then got out of the way for less than an hour. My phone rang, and I missed the call. It was Hunter. I went to the room, and no one answered the door. He was gone, just like that. I went down to the desk to get a key to his suite and see if the rumor mill at the hotel had any idea. The girl was new and didn't seem to know much.

His suite looked like it was hit by a storm. There were cigarette ashes and butts, glasses of alcohol, books, bottles, and trash everywhere—just chaos. The pillows were a mess, even on the sofa. I was in the room only an hour ago. It looked much more peaceful then. Now, it was just a mess. I was now more confused as to why they left this way.

Back in the lobby, when the evening staff started to come in, I heard the gossip. The front desk manager said that Hunter had soiled the bed on numerous occasions, but last night was the worst. I was told that one of the housekeeping staff came to speak to him, and Anita started yelling at him, accusing him of being a disgusting, old man who she could no longer tolerate. She yelled and screamed at him until he just sat in the chair with his head down. This was where I found him.

    I have no idea what was true about that story. I do know they were not happy that day. I had assumed he didn't write the piece he needed to, and they were fighting because of that. I had no clue really, but so quickly, he was gone. I felt so much compassion and sadness for him. For Anita, too, but Hunter and I had become friends, and now . . . he was gone.

    I wondered if I would ever hear from him again.

    Then his late-night/early-morning voicemails started about a week after his departure. At times, he was rambling on the phone, and I had no idea what he was saying. Some messages started mid-sentence as if when my voicemail picked up, he was already well into the conversation. I answered when I could. He wanted me to come there. He said that he needed help writing and wanted me there. He was relentless, calling constantly, and I started to wonder if maybe I should just take this journey. I needed to make a plan though. I didn't want to stay gone too long at first. I needed to visit, feel it out, and then decide if I was going to stay longer. I said I would only come for ten days at first. Then I could decide if I wanted to accept the job. He agreed, and off I went to the crazy world of HST and the Owl Farm.

4

"Freedom is something that dies unless it's used."
—HST

Deciding to fly to Aspen and be picked up from the snowy airport by Hunter was all very overwhelming. I spent most of the flight wondering about my decision-making capabilities. What was I even getting into? I had no idea. I realized somewhere near Denver that I had not asked many questions, like who else would be home, what would my days look like, what exactly my job was going to be.

A few nights before leaving, I had dreamt I was sitting on the floor by a large chair where Hunter was. Anita was sitting across the room on a sofa. They were explaining to me how I was going to be kept as a "human pet" for Hunter. He was petting my head in the dream, and I remember thinking I liked the job or could get used to it. I thought I would make it into a film through him, in this dream, so I thought playing the part of human pet would help me tap into my inner animal.

After that dream, I felt afraid or unsure of everything. I had spoken to Hunter before I left New Orleans and, during my layover, had made a quick call to his voicemail, telling him I was on time. I had heard him scramble to get the phone as I was hanging up, but I didn't want to talk yet. I was on the verge of buying a ticket back home at that point, and talking to him could have sent me there. Plus, I like getting voicemail—it suits me.

I never felt I would be in danger. I just felt like I was about

HELLO I'LL BE STEALING FROM YOU TODAY

to join a circus, and I wasn't so sure I was ready to perform in one where I was not even sure of my role. I knew that being around him in Nola was like a crazed traveling zoo and I knew my place in that, but that's out of town for him. It does things to people. Take a slightly bizarre person out of their home, and they will most likely be more bizarre. So, I thought Hunter at home would be more about business with a bit of drinking, too much serving, and some attempts at getting that piece we started working on for Playboy in on time.

My flight arrived in the evening, right after dark, to a small Aspen airport. I knew he wanted to personally come and get me, but I took this to mean that he and a driver of some sort would pick me up at the airport. The man was never sober, so I was sure someone would be aware and not send him to get me. I grabbed my luggage and called Hunter's main phone line. I got a pick up, followed by silence, yelling that sounded like a distressed puppy, and then a disconnection.

Not off to a good start.

I dialed the second phone line. It rang about three or four times, and then Hunter picked up. He sounded like he was on a treadmill or practicing yoga, out of breath and a bit erratic.

"Oh, Heather, you are safe," he says.

Why the fuck would I not be? I say, "Yes, I'm at the airport, outside with my bags, and you are home, answering your phone. Should I be looking for a car picking me up?" Then he starts yelling about people hiding his keys, being out to get him, not wanting us to be together, wanting him home, and taking his shit.

This rant is not making me feel great about this trip. I say that I am going to take a cab and need the physical address.

"Wait! Call me back on the other line in twenty seconds," he tells me. I hear confidence in his voice. I hang up and dread this next couple of weeks for a moment. What am I thinking?

Okay, dial the main phone again.

He is yelling at someone when he picks up, but that's okay because just hearing another voice there makes me feel a bit better. I once again suggest a cab. He is appalled.

"No," he barks at me. "I wanted to be there waiting for you, but they stole my keys, so I am stuck in this place. I've been searching since you called from Denver! Heather, I need to be there to get you!" He sounds pissed, he sounds a bit fucked up, he sounds deranged.

I say, "Okay, what the fuck then!?" I suddenly yelled it right into the phone at him. I'm freezing, standing outside at night, and I'm pissed off! He laughs because he likes that kind of shit—pissing people off.

Finally, someone takes the phone from him. This takes some convincing, but he gives in and hands over the phone. It's a female voice—I am hoping it's Anita. She says hello, that she is sorry for the confusion, she is Sally and will be coming to get me. She describes her SUV to me, and we hang up. I'm relieved that I will be getting there in the safety of this sane-sounding stranger.

About twenty minutes later, the airport is almost empty. I'm still standing outside, cold and stuck to the ground. I have hardly moved at all. The conversation I had with Hunter is going through my mind. I heard only some of what Hunter was saying, but it sounded like some sort of conspiracy to him. I wonder then if someone really did hide his keys. He wanted to be waiting here for me. Is that what I needed to see right off my uncertain flight? A very intoxicated man who has trouble walking when he's not drinking to excess, a person who cannot stand up without help, picking me up and driving me to his home?

I feel dazed and anxious when I see Sally heading over to where I am standing. When she gets out, I am delighted to see another girl. She's my age or a bit older and looks very sober and capable. She apologizes for the awkward moment over the phone, telling me Hunter loses his keys sometimes and then thinks someone took them. Good enough for me.

I'm with her now, driving up snowy mountains at night while she tells me the better points of the job I'm going to be taking over. She was assisting him until now, until my arrival, but she says that she can stay a few days while I get more accustomed to my surroundings. She offers to show me how to get to the grocery store, tells me she will stay until I feel comfortable. I like her already. I am relieved to know I won't be the only one with Hunter each day.

She says Anita is not home and not expected back for a while. I didn't know this when I agreed to come, but I have Sally and I'm okay with this. We will share this job and help each other while I learn more about what's going on. She lives a town over, so she will drive home nightly, and I will be in the famous guesthouse I have heard stories of. Johnny Depp stayed there for months to study Hunter for Depp's role in *Fear and Loathing in Las Vegas*. Kate Moss was also with him at the time. Sure, there are other stories about that guesthouse, but that is one of my favorites. Sleeping in the bed where Johnny and Kate were having hot sex was sure a perk!

As we drive through the gates of Owl Farm, I think this will all be fine. I think.

5

The second day starts quiet, tranquil even, and with Hunter sleeping extremely late into the afternoon, I have time to walk the grounds and enjoy the snow a little. I try to remind myself that I am here to work and I am here for Hunter, but I am in need of alone time. I have started to feel like a babysitter to an adult toddler. He needs help with everything, and my own body cannot help another body walk. I am hurt, too.

I walk around this morning feeling like today is a new day. I spoke to Anita on the phone earlier, and she will be coming home soon, either tonight or tomorrow. I am excited about this because I feel like it will help Hunter to have her around, but more than that, it will help me with Hunter. Sally will still be with us again tonight, so even if Anita doesn't get here today, I may not have to be left alone with him at all. I don't mind being alone with him, but I think it may be more than I can take.

I walk over to the main house after I'm done. I see that the housekeepers are there, so I go inside. Hunter is still asleep, so I make some lunch. I think I can handle the job when I return to Colorado later. Even though I will be living here for a few months if I accept the job, I will always have the afternoons to myself. Hunter sleeps late, and it will allow me to have some time to myself. As I am walking out of his house, I see a note with my name on the top. It reads:

Tues Jan 24, 05 (who knows what time of night it was written)

Heather,

HELLO I'LL BE STEALING FROM YOU TODAY

Come over and wake me up at 12:30 (scratched out the 12:30) 2:00 p.m.—or any time you wake up. Eat & drink whatever you want in kitchen. Pam should be here, expecting you. We will go into town tonight for gin, wisdom, etc.

Ok, see you soon, H

I ignore the part about waking him up, and I head over to the guesthouse to eat my lunch and think about this a bit more. We will be going into town, and Hunter will no doubt be behind the wheel of the jeep . . . I am not sure I like that idea. We are on a snowy hill, and town is at the bottom of this hill. On the other hand, I am getting a bit stir crazy on this secluded property and would love to go out and socialize. The X Games are here, and maybe there will be interesting people to see and meet. I am looking forward to getting out of the house, but I am glad it won't be just Hunter and I. Sally will be here and maybe even Anita. This could be fun.

Hunter finally gets up around 4 p.m. and calls the guesthouse immediately to tell me he is up and would like me to come into the house. I walk in and it is quiet—no TV, no music, just quiet. I enter the kitchen and spot Hunter sitting in there with his glasses perched on the end of his nose, silk robe on, hunched over with a cigarette in his mouth, reading the paper. He has a scotch on the rocks and a cup of coffee in front of him, and he looks at me over his glasses and gives me a quick grin. He continues reading, and I take a seat at the end of the kitchen counter. I have my notebook and start journaling while he continues to read. After about fifteen minutes, he puts the newspaper down and asks me if I have been up for long. I tell him I awoke around 1 p.m., and he wonders why I did not wake him. I explain that I felt like he might be tired after the handfuls of pills he took around

5 a.m. when I was going to bed and that I thought he might need to sleep it off.

He smiles. We have a bit more small talk about my stay, and we go over a few of the things he would like me to do over the next couple of days. I take notes, and my list includes the following:

- Organize pens into groups based on whether or not they are water-based or non-water-based. The pens need to be easier to find without all the added confusion.
- Await UPS package of forward from Sean Penn for HST's new book
- Thurs.—X Games begin, visitors will be calling.
- Tues. night—dinner with lawyers and Supreme Court
- Check with store about more Gonzo tank tops and t-shirts
- Wednesday—try to get shotgun art done
- Read article in *Vanity Fair* before dinner tonight.

This list is one of many random lists I would make during my stay. We rarely get all of the few things done that we set out to do, but it is nice to have a list of short-term goals, I suppose. Tonight, before going out, Hunter is going to a dinner party with some attorneys and a few Supreme Court justices. He hopes to convince a particular Supreme Court justice to help a wrongfully accused prisoner, or at least listen to the story. Hunter has been writing to Lisl and her family since her incarceration, and he believes she is innocent. He hopes the dinner party crowd will agree. The party is in Aspen, and he is taking Sally with him. She knows the area and can drive in the snow and get him home if he can no longer drive. I will get the house to myself tonight for a few hours—this is the best news I have heard in a few days! I can relax, drink wine,

HELLO I'LL BE STEALING FROM YOU TODAY

and cook whatever I can find in the many freezers of delicious food. After dinner, we are all going out to the tavern.

Later on, we will be expecting visitors to Owl Farm. Hunter is not sure who will be coming by during X Games. People always call to drop by, and this year he expects quite a few calls. I am excited. Aspen dinner parties should be even better than the celebrity dinner parties in New Orleans!

Hunter is in a great mood today and looking forward to the party. He asks my opinion on what he should wear, and we talk about the people who will be there. I read from *Fear and Loathing in Las Vegas*, and we discuss a few of the funnier points. He likes when I read to him because I don't just read the words but read like only an actor can, or so he says. I love reading to people. It is one of my favorite things to do.

Before Sally arrives, we get a phone call from Anita. I am happy to hear from her when I answer the phone, and I tell Hunter she is on the line. He picks up with a sudden scowl on his face. His side of the conversation is cold and angry, and I can tell immediately by his reaction that they are not getting along.

When he hangs up the phone, he gives me instructions. While he is sleeping or not home, she is not allowed in the house or the guesthouse under any circumstance. If she comes by, I must tell her she is not allowed inside unless he is home. I must set the alarm when he leaves and press the panic button at the sight of a car pulling into the long driveway.

FUCK! My peaceful relaxed night has just become very confusing and unsettling. I am ill-equipped to do this job, and he won't tell me why I am expected to keep her out. I don't even have a reason to give her except Hunter said so, and she has a key, so how do I stop her? I hate being in the middle of this and I really like Anita. Hunter's mood is now sour, and he wants to be alone, so I head to the guesthouse to figure out how the hell to keep Hunter's wife out of her own home while he is out . . .

6

FEAR . . . I have felt fear before in many different ways. This night with Hunter, I feel fear in too many ways for one civilized evening.

Through the beginning of the night, he acts as though he has forgotten about going out and forgotten about leaving the note at all. It was written in the late night or early morning before he went to bed, so he could have just forgotten. That is just fine with me because he has been drinking straight whiskey since about 2 p.m. It is now dark. We are trying to work and seem to be focused on an article he needs to finish.

Suddenly he remembers, just like that.

"We are going out tonight, going to the bar for drinks," he says to me with a smile. By now, Sally—each and every time she shows up, I say a little "AMEN!"—was also with us. I figure she has worked with him longer—if she is down for a little night out, then I am too. I am glad she is coming. I am comfortable with her. I also assume she will drive. This is an assumption we shared.

When it is time to leave, Hunter gets into the driver's seat of the jeep. Sally asks him, "Do you want me to drive so you can just sit back and relax?" Smart one.

But he is in the "absolutely not" zone, where we know there is no way around it—just get in and enjoy the fucking ride. She sits up front, and I sit in the back. I need her to have her eyes on the curvy, snowy road with him. He has a drink between his legs, overfilled and spilling on him. He has to grab it a few times and drink it down a bit to stop it from spilling all over him.

HELLO I'LL BE STEALING FROM YOU TODAY

The first few minutes... FEAR. Then I just have to say, "Fuck it. I'm here. I'm going down this mountain with this man right now, and if we crash, there is little to nothing I can do about that." I have a shot of whiskey and sit back to check out the scenery. At first, he drives pretty well. Then, he is excited and going downhill so fast, whipping around curves, drinking his cocktail, and looking at us while laughing, talking, I don't know. I am sure we are going to crash into the side of the mountain or just fall right off the side of this road. I just have to give in even more. I give into that thought and join the moment for a bit of the crazy laughter. This is an insane situation. I didn't really know either of these people that well, I have no idea where I am, and I can't control anything.

Down, down, down the mountain we go.

Somehow, we make it down. Thankfully, there are no cars coming up because I am pretty sure we were in both lanes most of the time. At the bottom, we just drive a couple of minutes to the tavern—Hunter's spot, the place he has gone for years. He parks in the no-parking space on the side of the building, and we walk in.

It is a tavern, a dive bar, and it is pretty quiet.

Most people are at the X Games parties, all of which we are invited to attend and I want to attend, but Hunter tonight did not. So, I belly up to the bar and start drinking—just Hunter and the two assistants from different worlds, talking about our lives and our homes. We talk a lot and have a really good time. A few more people come in, want to talk to Hunter too, and soon we have a small group of people talking and drinking.

After an hour or two, Anita walks in. I am so happy to see her. I have been waiting for her to come back since I arrived. I hug her and we grab a drink and go back to the table. Over the next few minutes, as I talk to Anita, I can sense tension. Hunter is not happy once more. He starts getting angry, and Anita is not really speaking to him much. I feel confused yet again.

She tells me that he does not like her coming, getting in the way of his time with me. But she says it like we are on a date—makes me feel like things just got weird. I tell her I am sure she just needs to talk to him. She says she has and she knows what he wants now.

She likes me. She is happy I am there. It feels like we are talking about me taking over some position she holds, and I feel odd. Fearful. What am I doing here? Am I here to help him write or here to be the new lady of the house? This is just too much.

Maybe I have had too much to drink and just misunderstood this whole thing. Maybe that's it.

Hunter is ready to go and not too happy. Anita disappears at some point. He asks her to leave a few times, but I am not sure when she actually leaves. When we walk out, he goes to the jeep and silently gets in and starts the engine. I say goodbye to someone and walk over to the jeep when it happens.

And now to set this fun little scene: Snowy night. The jeep is running. Hunter's in the driver's seat. Sally is behind him in the backseat this time. I walk toward them and have to step over a snowy, icy block that formed around the perimeter of the tavern, about a foot and a half wide. I step over with one foot, and the minute I pull my other foot over, I slip on the hard-as-fucking-shit ice. Immediately, I feel a burning, stinging, shocking pain and can't catch my breath. I have fallen in a way that puts me almost under the running jeep Hunter is in control of. My mind goes into a panic. I have to move, I feel like he's going to run me over. FEAR.

I yell in pain and in fear, and I hear Hunter yelling, "Get

her! Help her!"—something that made me want to just move out from under this jeep more. I scream as I stand up with the help of Hunter's sheriff friend, who is also in the parking lot watching all of this happen. Without the panic I am feeling, there's no way I can move my body off of that ice. I get to my feet and into the passenger's seat, crying from the searing pain in my spine. I know I need medical attention, but at this point, I cannot even find my breath to speak. Hunter puts his hand on my shoulder softly and asks if I am okay.

I shake my head no. I have no idea what to do.

He says we should head home, and he starts driving. I imagine another drive like the one before, but this time, he is very gentle and slow. He checks on me, seems very concerned, and keeps trying to get me to talk. I just want him to look at the road, so I get out a few words, and I just close my eyes. Tears are coming. I can't stop them, but it's dark, and I just keep quiet. He drives slowly and carefully all the way home. I need help getting out of the car and onto the sofa— I'm hurt way more than I let on. Since I deal with chronic pain daily, I'm a bit accustomed to dealing with pain and hiding it when I need to. I know, though, that they know it's bad because I am bruising already. Hunter says that since he was a "doctor," he is going to suggest I take two Percocets, drink another cocktail, and lie down. I do this and just hope nothing is seriously fucked.

After a few hours on the sofa in the main house, I want to go back to the guesthouse to sleep. Hunter says that I need better shoes, snowshoes, and has me wear some of Anita's boots. He comes outside and watches me walk into the guesthouse, making sure I do not fall again. I walk slowly, agonizing pain in my spine, wave goodnight, and go inside. Hunter is patient with me this night, taking care of me for once. He is fatherly and kind, a side of him I do not see very much of.

The next few weeks, I would be on anti-inflammatory pills and muscle relaxers, bruised badly, and would slowly go back to the normal level of pain I came here with. But that night, as I sleep, Anita comes into the guesthouse and leaves a note for me. Through the fall, pain, and pills, I had forgotten about the weird vibe in the tavern. I just thought it was in my head. I wake up the next day and slowly get out of bed to read a very strange letter from Anita.

The letter is folded up, written on yellow legal pad paper. It is three pages long. She used the back and front of each page and wrote notes in the margins. The notes look frantic, scribbled, as though written in anger or very quickly. The tone is not angry so I assume she was in a hurry to leave the letter and get off the property before we came home from the tavern. She wrote some personal things in the letter and then I can tell she read it again and added the notes in the margin to make sure I understand her side.

She said many things, but the overall message is that Hunter wants private time with me, and she was ruining that. It made him mad and, I think, it made her believe that I was going to be his new love interest. She is kind, respectful, and delicate with her words. It is clear that she only wants to be understanding toward Hunter. She wants him to be happy, and if he wants to be with me, we have her blessing.

I have no intention of being involved with Hunter in any way besides working with him, and I want her to know that right away. I want to put her mind at ease, from my end at least, that nothing is going on between us. But she isn't at the house, and I can't get in touch with her. She has allowed me into Hunter's life in a way I just am not ready for. I don't want to and don't think about at all, ever. I feel confused. I feel uncomfortable that he gave her that impression. Hunter has not said a word to me and has not crossed the boundaries of friendship and work, so I think at first maybe it is Anita just feeling a bit jealous. Only, she wrote that he had told her at the tavern that she was in the way, ruining some kind of private time with me. He had to have thought this was a possibility at least. I speak to her a couple of days later, and I assure her I was not at their home for anything but to work and to help Hunter and her as much as I can. She is very gracious but seems sad. There is much more going on between them at that time, and I am sure she is feeling a lot of mixed emotions.

So I just try to forget about it and move on with my job. I was there for a reason and it was nothing personal.

7

"Politics is the art of controlling your own environment."
—HST

Isolation station.

When I met Hunter, he came with a slew of celebrity friends, writers, and other interesting people I was happy to be around. I enjoyed working with him one-on-one, but also enjoyed getting out and meeting people in the field that I wanted to be working in. He kept me busy, and I enjoyed it.

Coming to Aspen during the X Games, just being here was exciting and filled me with expectation. I saw the invites to the private events and heard the messages on the answering machine requesting the number of people he would need on the guest list. We were invited everywhere! I was happy to stay in at first, but I also wanted to experience this place a bit from the VIP area! Going out to parties sounded fun, but when I brought it up to Hunter, he changed the subject, got annoyed. He knew I was not a celeb psycho or just wanting to go for any weird reasons, so why was he being so odd? I later heard him on the speakerphone, getting a personal invitation from a restaurant owner for us to attend a dinner in his honor, followed by drinks in the adjacent bar. He alluded to our busy schedule and said he would see what we could do. What the fuck? I wanted to be returning these calls, accepting these invites, enjoying this place a bit! I was getting a bit sick of this isolation and needed to see other humans.

At some point during the few days of my pouting about

HELLO I'LL BE STEALING FROM YOU TODAY

missing a spectacular private event, I mentioned the snow had slowed, and I wanted to go down to the grocery store to get some food and just take a short drive. The jeep sitting there was supposed to be for me to use if needed, and I needed! By midday, Hunter had filled our time completely with mundane bullshit and, by the end of the day, had me write a list of groceries for the housekeeper to pick up for me on her way in. This was starting to feel very claustrophobic. I asked, "Is it because of the snow? I can drive. The roads have been cleared, and I have directions. I'm quite capable."

"Nope, just wanted you here today. We are very busy."

"I organized pens at your desk for an hour. WE are not busy!"

The next few days were more of the same, social events we should have been attending, declined for no reason. I mentioned that maybe we could just pick one event, the best one or the least crowded or whatever, and just get out. He was pissed at me, I could tell. I went back to the guesthouse and got pissed, too.

Maybe it was him—the hip replacement, back and leg pain, his inability to walk, and him thinking people would think he is just this old, broken man. I felt bad for him because I knew what it was like to be in constant pain. I don't know what it was like for people to expect a certain level of crazy and to feel unable to deliver. Maybe this was just him feeling uncomfortable. I went back to the main house, and we talked, cooked lobster, and wrote a bit of random shit.

Back in my room that night, I thought about things. I realized he just didn't want to go out. He didn't want me to leave either—at all. It was about me leaving this place for any reason, to go to the store or to just get out. I had not left the gates since I was driven in over a week before—with the exception of going with him to the tavern. It was time for me to get out, even just for a bit.

I called Sally the next morning. It was sunny and beautiful outside, and Hunter was asleep. The housekeeper was here for another couple of hours, so I asked Sally if we can please go for a fucking drive. I needed out! Please! She was surprised I hadn't left, saying the jeep keys were there for me so I could leave if I needed. I had not seen these keys at all. Come over now please!

I figured we would be back long before his usual wake-up time in the afternoon, so it was no big deal, and besides, I was a grown-ass woman!

Sally picked me up, and I finally got a glimpse of this place in the daylight hours. The first thing she said was, "I cannot believe you didn't get the keys to that jeep. It was brought here especially for you, taken from an employee he fired the day you arrived. She was a friend of Anita's and suddenly could not be trusted by Hunter." So, after years of being his accountant and whatever other odd jobs he threw her way, he fired her suddenly. He had her bring the company jeep back to the house for my use.

Well, this was news to me. I wasn't sure what to say, but I felt like I was seeing another side of Hunter, a more personally anxious, crazed side. I wanted to enjoy the day, so I blew it off. Maybe we were getting more work done than I realized, and he felt like he needed me there. I told her I never felt stuck or felt the urge to leave on my own really. With all the recent snow, I was fine staying inside. This urge just came up as the sun started to shine. I also mentioned those parties and events for the X Games, the neglected fun. She gave me a concerned look and said that seemed strange to her. He had wanted to attend some of these events, as far as she knew. He was even participating in one!

HELLO I'LL BE STEALING FROM YOU TODAY

Okay, I just wanted to drop this for now. I needed to take in the scenery, breathe the fresh air.

The beauty of this place immediately blew my mind. It was pristine, bright white everywhere I looked, and our little roadway was cleared. The enormity of these mountains hit me . . . I was in the middle of nowhere. Woody Creek was at the end of the road, and we turned as Sally showed me the tavern in the daylight hours, the post office, and a few other small businesses lining the Main Street. Wow . . . small but lovely.

We headed toward Aspen, through the white wonderland of mountains, million-dollar homes jutting out of them. We snaked through the mountains, and Sally told me about some of the famous owners of those estates built into the tops of the hills and mountains. Everything seemed perfectly clean and bright white. I had seen snow before this in Seattle and New York, but nothing compared to this stunning view.

We finally arrived in Aspen, a pretty small town with very wealthy, well-dressed locals and tourists walking around and shopping or eating in old hotel restaurants. Sally and I drove around the main square as she told me about the well-known real estate there, and we looked around, sightseeing from the car. After a few turns around the square, we parked and walked. There were designer clothing stores and wonderful old hotels mostly, sort of a mix of shopping in LA and old Nola hotel history. It was a great day, and we lost track of time.

Sally left her phone in her car, and mine was at the house so we were not to be disturbed on our walk. By the time we got back to the car, she had seven or eight voicemails from Hunter within the last hour. He sounded nervous, afraid and unsure of what to do. He didn't know where I could be. Where else would I be? I didn't know anyone else here!

She called him, to ease his mind, but was very quick with him. She said, "Heather needed to get out, and we were having a good time, walking around the shops in Aspen. We won't be long." He was yelling, but she stopped him and just said, "We will be back soon. Everything is fine."

When she hung up, I was ready to head back to his home. But once she said she wanted to show me the place where she liked to go for ski apparel and equipment, I wanted to go. She is a ski instructor, I liked talking to her, and I felt really good. Hunter would be fine.

An hour or so went by, and we were ready to leave. Back in her car, she had more voicemails from Hunter about getting me back there now! Now she seemed a bit more concerned and decided we should go back with some of his favorite treats—hot dogs from a vendor in Aspen. Okay, let's bring the swine. It's going to be interesting.

The drive back made me wish I were flying over the place in a helicopter, really taking it in. Made me want to see more beauty. I'm a beach girl, but this was wonderful because after the snow stopped falling and the sun came out, it wasn't too cold. It was beautiful and manageable for someone like me who likes to be warm.

Sally decided she would come inside and stay a while when we got back. This was great, but what the fuck was going on? Why was I feeling like there was more to this, more to me being there with no way out? I didn't say much more about it. I didn't want her to say anything to Hunter and make him think I felt I was trapped, a prisoner in his guesthouse. I didn't want that. I just wanted to know why I had no option to leave and why he was so upset when I did leave.

With Sally there, the evening was pretty normal. He said something about being worried, said I should leave a note if I am going to leave. I tell him that I'm sorry. I'm not accustomed to checking in with anyone if I am going on a little sightseeing drive, but that I did tell Pam, the housekeeper.

He was happy about the hot dogs, I was happy Sally was staying with us, and we were all in good spirits by the time the sun was setting.

But I think his revenge for my leaving the house came later that night when I was introduced to the late-night swimming pool outing.

First shitty thing: it was cold! It was late, snowing, and the pool was not on the property but down the street at the home of a friend of Hunter's.

Then I was introduced to the rule about robes. Only robes are to be worn to the pool—pick one from behind the bathroom door and take off everything else. This pool did not allow clothing, according to Mr. Hunter.

This pissed me off, mostly because it was freezing! Sally came into the bathroom and said, "Just roll up your pant legs and roll your shirt sleeves up under the robe. He won't notice, and you can just put your feet in the water." She said she does it all the time.

I told him I didn't want to go, it was stupid, it was late, it was snowing, and I was cold.

He said he needed me to come because he went there for water therapy, and I needed to be able to take him there when Sally was not here.

FUCK THIS!

Then . . . Okay, clothing under robe, let's go.

Again, he was walking and using Sally and I as his own walking stick. He pressed down on my shoulders, and it hurt. He knew damn well I had a terrible spine, so what was this? Some stupid fucking punishment.

We drove three houses down, the route I needed to know, yeah, okay. Then it was time to get out into the snow and ice and walk in the dark to this house with all of the lights out in the middle of the night and get inside safely with this crazy, loud man.

Once inside the family home, I was not convinced we were even allowed to be here. It seemed like we are breaking in or something. Through the dark, huge home, we made our way to the doorway leading to the indoor heated pool. On the way, Hunter stepped on a child's toy, causing him to yell and curse.

I could only be thankful again for Sally, who took over helping him walk after she saw I could not do it. I really was glad she was here once again.

The indoor pool area was beautiful, windows all around, fogged up but I could still see the view. Snow was falling, and white mounds were collecting along the sides of the house. Hunter disrobed, jumped into the water, and swam around. We both laughed. Sally told me that during the times Hunter was underwater swimming, that this was what she did—sit on the side and put her feet into the water. He was happy with that. She told me the owner of the house was an old friend of Hunter's and gave him permission years ago to swim anytime he wanted. I bet he didn't expect these 4 a.m. swims! The man's wife was not so happy about the arrangement, but it was okay for now.

When the swim was done, I was exhausted. Luckily, so were Hunter and Sally.

8

> *"I wouldn't recommend sex, drugs or insanity for everyone,
> but they've always worked for me."*
> —HST

Insanity . . . that's the word I feel will best describe the evening I just endured. And insanity does work for Hunter somehow. He can pull off all sorts of insane things that most people would be arrested if they attempted.

Like with guns . . . he likes the guns.

I had heard some stories before my arrival at Woody Creek—Hunter accidentally shooting another assistant a few years ago. He also may or may not have tried to shoot a person in his home as a joke (The joke being that the bullet would go right over the person's head. Ha, ha . . .), and he is just known for being an avid shooter of fucking guns. For reasons known only to him, when he gets in any mood, the gun expresses the mood the best. In his younger days, when he could walk a bit steadier and move about with ease and a bit of grace, he could shoot those guns most times without causing a great deal of panic among those near him. He knew what he was doing, did it often, and was sure of himself.

At this point in time, however, he is not that person. He has become older and has trouble with pain and pain pills. Alcohol and pain pills and lacking ability to walk, leaning on furniture to move, leaning on my shoulder to walk—all of these things did not make me feel at ease if a gun were to show up during my visit. I figured he'd bring it out regardless, but just during the day. We were supposed to make "gun art" in the yard out of some garbage cans for the X Games, and that was what I expected—protected shooting with others nearby and in daylight, mostly outside.

Being that insanity seemed to work for him, he came home from a very important dinner with some attorneys and some people who work closely with Supreme Court justices, CEOs of major companies, etc.

Now, hours later, he returns home after the one night I actually got to sit down, watch TV a bit, and eat some food alone in the quiet snowy darkness. I had a peaceful night so far, but Hunter is home, and he is in a good mood. A very good mood. So good that he immediately comes into the house and starts talking about how great everything went, and it seems like that pure child-like excitement only he can exude.

He walks into the kitchen, where I had taken my perch at the stool at the end of the kitchen bar. He walks deeper into the kitchen to his post where he usually sits and has a drink while we talk, write, and read. He puts his hand under the part of the kitchen bar he usually sits at and pulls out his handgun—with a smile that says to me, "I'm fucking crazy. Get out of the way!" I am immediately nervous as I always am around guns, and he can tell. But he is on a fucking roll. He's looking through me, and he is on a mission!

He starts to walk toward me, leaning on the kitchen counter while stumbling along, gun in hand. I'm afraid and trying to stay out of the direct path of the gun. That's all I could see—Hunter, walking as if he will fall any minute, yelling like a madman, holding this gun, and using it to hold himself up. He makes it to where I am standing rather quickly and puts his arm on my shoulder to lean on me.

That gun, the fucking gun. That's all I see. The hand

holding the gun moves carelessly around, making it hard for me to both help him walk and stay out of the gun's trajectory. I'm sure he is going to shoot me by some accident or shoot himself whenever we make it to wherever we are going. He looks insane enough to have eaten someone's soul. I kid you not. It is like he had just gotten a blood transfusion from Keith Richards.

We walk as carefully as possible to the next room and then outside to a small balcony. When we make it to the door, he tries opening it with the hand that has the gun. I have to just do this shit so we can get where we are going. I can't keep up with him and watch the gun any longer. Whatever we are doing, I am in, like it or not. He is a crippled steam engine.

At the balcony, he lets go of me and walks to the railing. I immediately take a few steps back into the darkness and into a cage of fucking flamingos I did not notice before. Was this new? Suddenly, I hear shots, and I'm not sure I want to look. By the time I do look over, he is shooting again, this time into the sky, and has started yelling like a crazy man. He is out of control. I stand as close to the door as possible to get away from him. I know all about falling bullets from the news in New Orleans on New Year's Eve. "Falling bullets kill," they always remind you on television.

Yes, they do indeed.

This goes on for what feels like twenty minutes, but most likely is closer to three or four, I would guess. He stops, laughing and saying something I can't hear. He listens to the silence, laughs like a madman, and then starts shooting again. I think he loads a couple of times. I'm not really worried any longer about him shooting himself or me, but I start to get really worried about the walk back inside with Mr. Trigger Happy.

After he unloads, he turns to me with a smile as big as my

fear. He asks me if I want a turn while holding the gun toward my belly. NO, FUCK NO!

"No, thank you. Let's get inside. I really hate guns," I say. He laughs again, shoots again. He is done.

But is the gun still loaded? I have no idea. He had just pointed it at me and then shot one more time, so there was something left, right? His eyes are wide as his smile. This is fun to him. I feel afraid and confused.

The entire way back to his kitchen, I try my best to help us both get there safely, so we can just sit the fuck down and have a cocktail. He wants that, too, so I have him on the hook! Walking back, the gun is carefree, loosey goosey. As he holds my shoulder with one hand, that gun just flops around in his free hand. He uses it as an extension of his arm to hold onto the sofa, the doorway, the table. Finally back in the kitchen, he asks me again if I'm sure I don't want to shoot?

"No, thank you. I want to hear about your night tonight and have that drink." That's a good way to get him off one subject and on another—just let him know you're interested in what he has to say, which I was, and bring out the drinks.

The gun is safely tucked away under the kitchen bar where he sits each and every day. I know it is there now, and it could make an appearance at any moment. I am nervous whenever he reaches around that drawer. After a few hours, we are back to normal, sitting and talking about the night and going over notes to fax the next day. I never really thought he would hurt me on purpose, but I did have the feeling that night for a fleeting moment that he might hurt himself or hurt me by accident.

His face is more normal now, happy and a bit dazed over, but not so erratic. He feels better, more relaxed after shooting this gun into the dark night, into whatever was across the street. It gave him some of the feeling of being his old self, I think, to just get up and shoot when he wanted to. He liked it, and he respected guns and hunters.

I have had a better understanding of the hunter mentality after talking to him. He has taught me about population control and respecting the animals you hunt, a different take than I had heard in the South. It was just the fact that when he is having a hard time standing up straight, walking on his own, and have been drinking all day and night, then the gun in hand was scary. Leaning wrong on the trigger and then . . .

Getting shot by accident by an avid shooter in his home? No, this is not for me.

9

"Buy the ticket, take the ride . . . and if it occasionally gets a little heavier than what you had in mind well . . . maybe chalk it off to forced conscious expansion: Tune in, freak out, get beaten."
—HST (*Fear and Loathing in Las Vegas*)

If I were in an insane asylum, at some point I think I would just have to embrace the craziness and let go, be one of them. At Hunter's house, I felt this way one fine day. I woke up and thought it was time for me to quit being a little bitch and be part of this crazy man's world. After everything that we had done, it was time for me to really be there. I was feeling brave, I was going to do whatever he asked this particular evening. If he offered me Chivas, cocaine, pills . . . I was going to take the ride with him. I didn't tell him this. I wasn't fucking insane yet. But I told it to myself, and I was going to try to go down the rabbit hole a bit.

That evening when he offered me a drink and I accepted, he looked surprised, intrigued, that "eyes looking over the rim of the glasses with a smile" look . . . and we started reading and drinking. I was reading *The Rum Diary* that particular evening, and I was having fun with it. We talked about the story, the reality, and the book. He helped me to better understand his thought process as a writer. He was intimidating at times, but he was really talking that night, and so was I. He told me some of his stories of being a young, hungry journalist. We talked about drugs and the role they can play in the creative process. I told him I think it's impossible to really know yourself unless you have been on hallucinogenic drugs at least once. He laughed that infectious laugh and clapped his hands, cigarette dangling from his lips. The wall was down, and we were having fun. He was my friend that night—we were having an evening as friends, and that was completely different than any time I arrived in Colorado (in Nola we were very much on friendly terms).

The focus shifted to me, my history, who I was. He suddenly needed to know all about my life. We were still drinking quite a bit, so he had me talking about my adventures in the Deep South—life in the country, eating mushrooms from cow shit, taking massive amounts of LSD. Then being young in New Orleans, where debauchery is a way of life. We talked about cocaine a bit—I was on a break from it. At some point, our conversation moved to the topic of guns.

I still didn't want to shoot a gun, and on a normal day, I wouldn't want to touch a gun. But this was not a normal day—it was Buy the Ticket, Take the Ride Day.

He took the gun out from beneath his kitchen counter/desk and started trying to tell me about safety. He wasn't really making me nervous this time, as it was in his hand and pointing away from me. He wanted me to hold it, to see how it felt. I talked around it, not really saying yes or no, just trying to get on to any other subject. This strategy worked slightly when I asked him about this cocaine-crushing apparatus he had. I had not seen this thing before; it was a little grinder that you put cocaine in, turn, and out comes dusty, pure cocaine, soft and easy to use. I think he had it since the late seventies.

We talked about that a bit, but the gun stayed out in front of him. We took a few Polaroid pictures, and we read some more. After a while, I realized this gun topic was not going away.

I had a few more drinks.

Okay, fuck it, I thought. Give me the gun. He laughed, asked me if I was sure and all that bullshit. No, I'm not fucking sure. Just do it before I change my mind! He gave it to me. We were still talking about something, but my mind wondered to what it must be like to put one of these in your mouth and shoot. How insane that must be . . . A premonition?

I handed him the Polaroid camera and had him take my photo with the gun, holding it facing away from me. He was proud I was holding it and thought maybe we could shoot soon. I then had him take another picture, but this time I put the barrel of the gun in my mouth. I'm not sure what came over me, I just did it. I held it there and felt the weight of it, the fucking fear. He snapped the picture, and I realized my finger was holding the trigger with a bit more force than I meant to.

I was done—gave it back to him and was freaked the fuck out. I was sure there was a safety on that gun, but I couldn't ask. I didn't really want to know if I had almost accidentally shot myself in the mouth while Hunter photographed it. I wanted to move on. Drink? Yes!

We needed to talk about something else, and he had mentioned reincarnation earlier that evening. I started to talk about ghosts, past lives, and future lives. We decided I was an "old Hollywood actress who will step on your toes or your face to get to the top." I am from the past, and he is reincarnated as his personality choice, "a horny, sex-crazed teenage girl, curious about everything." But we could both be drag queens, too. We laughed and dressed up a bit, dancing around as much as two people with lots of pain can.

Then the cocaine grinder made another appearance. He snorted the shit about twice an hour as long as I had been around him. He offered me some this time, having usually taken a bump and put it away. Okay, let's go!

This was not ordinary cocaine—it felt clean and felt pretty great. Pure adrenaline. He told me this was his "medicinal cocaine," whatever that may be. It was nice. The high lasted a really long time, and we talked about everything. I felt like a teenage girl at a slumber party—a deranged teenage girl at a colossally fucked-up slumber party—but it was silly and kind of delightful.

We prank called some celebrities, talked to a few, and he told me some fucked-up Jack Nicholson stories, one involving the detached head of an animal at his front door. He told me all about some certain high-ranking government officials with their own stash of medicinal cocaine.

At the end of the night, he asked me if I wanted to go into the hot tub room. This was a room right outside of the office, you could easily miss the door. It was a room with windows and a very hot Jacuzzi tub right in the middle. This didn't feel weird or sexual. It felt like a friend asking a friend to sit in the hot water and watch the snow fall outside of the big windows. So I said okay.

I went in first, after a bit of cocaine and a fresh cocktail. It was beautiful in that room. I could have stayed in that place alone all night. I don't normally like sitting in boiling hot water much, but the snow falling outside made it feel welcoming. He opened one of the glass doors, and we could see the snowy outside air mixing with the steam from the hot room. We both were pretty silent in there, just speaking about the beauty of the view. At one point, we saw what I thought was a dog, but Hunter said was a fox, a very large fox, seemingly nearby and interested in coming into our warm room. I was nervous. This was all new to me—the nighttime snow, the mountains surrounding us, the isolation, the darkness. I suddenly felt very much like prey to the wildlife outside the door and to the wild man I had befriended.

Once we were dry and back in the kitchen, the sun was starting to rise. I needed to rest, the heat from the water and the craziness of the night had exhausted me. Hunter didn't want me to go, as usual, and said, "Before you go, I have an offer."

Shit . . . okay, what?

"Would you like to take this LSD with me? I've had it since the late seventies, and I was never sure when to take it," he said. This was my night to do anything, and I smiled, thinking how crazy we would be, dancing around like two insane fucks in the morning sun on his old-ass potent LSD. Mr. Broken Hip and Ms. Shattered Spine, putting on a show!

He showed me the sealed container, old and weathered. I was flattered that he would offer this to me after holding onto it all this time. I also got the feeling he was not going to be around much longer. For a split second, I saw that realization in his eyes.

I saw the sun peeking over the horizon, and I realized my day of saying yes had ended. It was a new day.

"Thank you, but I can't go any longer. I'm exhausted. I would be no good to you for days if I took that. But thank you," I said.

Then he hugged me. He did this often. He was a person who liked to touch—hands, arms, my collarbone. Hugs were common. But this was sad and ominous. It felt like a goodbye.

I thought it was just the long night and started to leave. He tried to give me the Polaroid of me holding the gun in my mouth. I told him to keep it. I didn't want to look at that photo again. He said, "Are you sure? It'll be a good memory for you." He wanted me to have it.

I shook my head, and he tacked it onto the large lampshade in front of him.

At the doorway, I stopped and said, "Goodnight. I had fun with you." He smiled but looked so sad. I had to go . . . it was all too much.

I went to the guesthouse, and when I slept, I dreamt of wild dogs hiding in the trees, of a hungry fox, of guns firing, of the white snow swallowing me.

I awoke to phone calls from a frantic Anita, saying I needed to check on Hunter—something . . . something was wrong. He had taken more pills than usual, and wouldn't wake up when the housekeeper tried to get him out of bed. He did not turn in the full article she was expecting. She wanted to edit it and get it in immediately, and he was not waking up. Later that day, he laughed about anyone worrying about him.

10

I will take many of his secrets to my grave. But the stories I share are because they are from the journal entries of my time with Hunter, and he read much of them after I wrote them. He convinced me to allow him to read some of my writing, and the journal was the only thing I had with me.

Both Hunter and I felt rebellious and like we didn't fit in often, something we realized early in our friendship. We both felt intense anxiety and chronic pain, and we were both writers who were afraid to share our work with the world at times. Vulnerable. I think this is part of the reason he chose me to become his muse, his writing assistant, his talking buddy, his companion, and his employee. We recognized a sameness in each other, and we knew the look, and both went with it. We bonded right away, and that's not something I do often.

When he was in New Orleans, I felt more in control and comfortable. I was able to open up to him more and talk honestly about things I didn't usually talk about. He had a way of drawing things out of me, and it felt fine and natural. The fact that I had just met him didn't really matter at that time. We were on neutral territory when we met. A hotel, people coming in and out all the time . . . we weren't really alone. That made it easier to just open up, and the fact that I was talking to a man who spoke to some very interesting people on a daily basis and yet found my life, my story, interesting was a big deal. He took me into his world quickly and without hesitation, and I took that seriously. I treated it with respect and dignity.

Once I was in Aspen, in his home, the dynamic shifted

a bit. Though I had the famous guesthouse to myself, I felt always under his control. If our time together had started this way, I'm not so sure I would have agreed to travel and stay at Owl Farm. But I still enjoyed my time there. He was always questioning, always looking for his next story. He was a character, just being around him, reading out loud to him so many nights for so many hours . . . I learned a lot about him. The parts of the stories he had me read again or pauses or the laughter . . . all of it taught me a little bit about who he was.

He spoke slowly, choosing his words in a careful way, and it brought my attention right to him. The way he spoke made you assume he was about to impart wisdom on you that you would need. Now, later, whenever . . . you would need it.

At times, he was, to me, a child, a father figure, a lunatic, a mentor, a friend, a genius, a mix of these. He said what he was thinking, always. He may have almost killed me three times in our time together, but the key word is "almost." He was on a mission to kill himself, and I sensed it more than once. He spoke of "endings" often—when we watched his documentary, watched the news and talked of his ending of interest in it (especially George W. Bush), when we talked about the end of his writing, how difficult it is at times. Sad how clearly we can see in hindsight.

I only hope he finally found that thing that his heart sought.

11

I've mentioned before that reading out loud dramatically was one of my favorite parts of my job at Owl Farm. It felt like I was an actress reading a script written by the writer, allowing me full access to his characters' thoughts and ideas. We both enjoyed it, and we were a good pair—he said he could listen to me read to him for days without stopping, and I love reading aloud to an audience of one or one hundred. He loved hearing those words he wrote in another time, as another version of himself.

At times he would laugh out loud with his whole heart and body at an obviously silly part. Other times, he would giggle to himself at an inside joke or a thought provoked by these words I read and he had written. He often just looked straight ahead, imagining the scene taking place right there in the room, looking serious, a cigarette dangling on his lips. He would have me slow down at times or back up and start a paragraph again so he could hear it, like for the first time, again and again. He was a very captive audience and always listened with as much intensity as he spoke. I have never again had the pleasure of reading someone's words to them as they sit and listen with complete concentration. It was a great thing to see and do. That was some of my favorite times with him. Pure joy!

My last night with him, I spent a good amount of the late night hours reading before writing.

Finally he was ready to submit the article he was working on, the one that we should have sent in days ago. We wrote fragmented, random sentences . . . he laughed at the absurdity. Said the editor would love this and should have to work, damn it! We sent in a choppy, unfinished piece with an arrow he drew at the bottom, the line ending mid-sentence, as though there were more pages coming. Then he had me fax it just like that, with the idea that whoever received this would wonder where the subsequent pages were. He thought it was hilarious. I was just glad to have finally sent in some words.

Before the sun stared rising for the next day, I told him I needed to sleep. I was leaving later that day and was exhausted. He asked me to stay, and I reminded him that another assistant was arriving tomorrow and would stay until I returned. He was not happy. He was quiet. I said, "I will be here again, soon. I will call you when I get home." He was like a child losing a friend, sullen and fragile-looking when I walked out. I almost turned around. I felt so odd. As I was walking out of the kitchen into the next room to exit the home and go to sleep, he stopped me.

He asked, "Heather, I will see you again?"

I said, "Yes, for sure. I will be back here."

He looked at me with intense sadness in his eyes and said simply, "If I don't see you again, I will . . ." He trailed off, so I went and hugged him again.

I tried to reassure him that I would be back. He seemed to think I wouldn't be. Or he knew he would not be there by the time I was heading back.

He knew. He had it all planned. The family visit he wanted was lined up, all very carefully put together. It needed to happen a certain weekend. I heard him planning this many times, making sure it was going to happen.

He knew as he was watching me leave that he was going to shoot himself in that same kitchen, in that same chair, just a couple of weeks later. He was going to shoot himself with that gun we played with. He was going to do it before he had to continue to sit and suffer in pain. Unable to function, unable to write, unable to go out, unable to be himself.

He was already gone.

The next day, the phone was full of voicemails . . .

"Where is the next page? They only had one . . . what happened?" Confusion and obvious frustration was in Anita's voice. I assumed we had sent it to a faceless editor. I felt awful that we sent it to Anita. She was able to pull it together, though, and finished the article using his words when possible, trying to explain it all. She saved it for him, as she probably had done more often than anyone knew. He found the stress of it all very funny the next day.

I spoke to him briefly before I left for the airport, and he asked me again to stay. I promised him I would return, reminded him this was supposed to be a short visit, a trial run. I needed to make sure I could do this job. He did not beg me, but he was very intense in his request. He needed me there, he said. I assured him I would return. His mind was away, distant. He was the fatherly version of himself. Gave me some pocket money and told me a few little words of wisdom. He hugged me tight. He told me, among other things, to always carry a $100 bill in my wallet, hidden. He said I would need it one day and be happy it was there, and then he gave me a bill to put away, just in case. I still have it.

When I left, he held my hand tight and for a bit longer than I would have expected. His hands were old, knuckles large, and I know that hand when I see or feel it. The hand of a man who has lived.

The night he shot himself, I was sleeping, and I felt those same hands, his hands, on top of mine as I lay in bed.

Goodbye, sir.

"It gave me a strange feeling, and the rest of that night I didn't say much, but merely sat there and drank. Trying to decide if I was getting older and wiser, or just plain old."

—HST (*The Rum Diary*)

broken girl

1

Curtain goes up on another day.

Only, now you need to realize that she is gone forever, and you are left with me.

Who? You. That's who. All of it is you.

Pain first hit my body in angry drive-by shootings, sudden and unprovoked. I could have a good day and then feel as though my nerves in my legs were suddenly under attack, being smothered by my hip joints and bones. Or I could get a quick feeling of pain in my back, and it would last a few awful minutes, only to go away slowly and then laugh as it sneaked back into my body.

After my odyssey with Hunter and Hurricane Katrina, I continued with my regular life. I had been trying to get healthy. I wanted to practice yoga since I came from a background of ballet and craved movement. I wanted to eat better, drink less, party less, and I was starting to do these things. What I didn't expect is that I didn't feel much happier, or much of anything. I loathed being in social situations with too many people I did not know. I liked having very close friends but couldn't understand how to keep those friendships close. I was going deep inside my own mind, and my own body was taking me prisoner. The pain was taking me away little by little.

2

As the years go by, my body fails me faster and faster.

It all came eventually, the surgery, the pain that crept up slowly over the years. My discs breaking down, one by one, until multiple discs were worn away. Stenosis, arthritis (osteo and rheumatoid), nerves being compressed by everything, and then leg and foot pain that won't allow me to stand for more than a few minutes at a time. Sickness eating away at healthy tissue, making it harder each week to walk, move, shop, clean the house, do anything really.

This was all building up for years without my awareness, the bone death machine—scoliosis. I ignored the back pain at first. I hid, I lied, I pretended it was okay. The pain was there, but I could push it back into those hidden parts of my mind. I did more activities each day just to prove to myself or my spine that I could. I walked, ran, never stopped moving because if I stopped I might never start again. I said it would get better and downplayed the symptoms. My ability to push through it and to keep going was something I was proud of. Maybe I was doing too much then and just making the process of spinal breakdown happen faster. Or maybe I was just living as much as I could because I had to. Maybe I knew I wouldn't be able to forever. Either way, doesn't matter now as I lay in bed hurting from lying in bed.

Doctors prescribed pills—anti-inflammatory pills, pain pills, muscle relaxers, anti-anxiety pills—it was necessary, so very urgent for me to do SOMETHING before it progressed anymore, any faster. Let's try to slow this down a bit with medication, they said. Then we will see what can be done.

I rarely took the meds. My old self would take the pills and maybe enjoy it. But this is not that body, not that person. This is a falling-apart body, and pharmaceuticals are to numb the pain, stop the anxiety and depression.

I only took them when the pain was so out of control nothing else would work. By then, the medication was a joke compared to the pain level, and I was in the hospital often. I was fighting this like I could win, but I was losing the fight and losing my body.

My functioning, dancing, party-all-night body . . . in the ER, crying, unable to lie on the bed because the pain is everywhere. My legs, back, feet, hips all hurt. My hands and feet are always cold and bluish-purple. This is new.

I wake up, unable to move my legs, my back soaked in sweat. I am afraid, my heart is pounding, and my ears are on fire. Everything inside of me is setting off alarms, and pain is everywhere. I roll over and take my pain medication. Mild, but it takes some of it away. I feel like I have been run over.

A few nights later . . . deeply depressed. Sad and disappointed in myself, my mind, and body. I am weak, and I'm going to forever be weak.

A week goes by . . .

Shopping at a whole foods store, I have a spasm in my spine, and it goes into my groin and down my legs. It hurts and burns, and I need to scream. I am having trouble doing regular daytime life shit now. I just keep going, like I can make it go away by not looking at it. But then I start to scream.

I wake up at 4 a.m. screaming. I feel like I'm dying. I leave in an ambulance and go to a hospital, where doctors and nurses tell me very little. I need to see more doctors—this much is clear. I get a needle to the hip, and the pain goes back into its hiding spot for a bit.

I continue to wake up screaming, not knowing it is my

own voice, thinking at first it is someone else. I scream at times when I go from sitting to lying down or standing to sitting. I cry when I sat in the car after work, unable to ignore the throbbing and shooting lightning pain in my back and legs. Screaming and crying at home, working and going to college, hanging out with friends when possible. It is crashing down on me, and I just know it and ignore it completely.

Four months pass, and I'm at the doctor's office panicking yet again. I cry. I am hurting inside my body and my mind. Did I do this to myself? Did I get so fucked up that my body and mind have turned against me? The pain is growing like some monster inside of me that can't be tamed.

Tests, more tests. Then waiting. Then Valium. My heart rate and blood pressure are off-the-charts high, I'm afraid to know, but I need to know.

The doctor goes over my results, telling me about my spinal canal not being large enough for the nerves that run through it. It's closing in on the nerves. I have herniated discs, bulging discs, and general nerve damage throughout my body. The leg pain is coming from the nerves, mostly. I have a bone disease. My mind goes out of the room at this point. I can't listen anymore. I know I'm nodding my head, but I have no clue what is coming out of this doctor's mouth. I'm lost, anxious, not getting air . . . then suddenly, blackness. Nothing, an instant reprieve from all of the pain . . . the light turned off.

When I regain consciousness, I am lightheaded, confused. The bright light pierces my eyes. I think I dreamed that conversation with the doctor because now there is someone else looking down at me. I look at her, and then the doctor walks back in. Fuck, this is my reality. I'm falling to little pieces, I'm a cookie crumbling, and I blame myself. I did this.

I leave with some knowledge about my conditions, but don't pay attention to much of it. I know at one point he had a piece of paper with a list of spinal conditions on it. He was going to circle the ones I was going to need to learn more about. But then he decided it would be easier to just scratch off the few I don't have to deal with. He's marked off three or four. The rest are mine to keep.

Well isn't this a lot of great news? I'm drained, confused, angry, and spinning. I fill some medications at the pharmacy and sleep for six months.

I just existed and felt sorry for what I had become. I was now a recluse. I didn't want to leave the house. I didn't do much or try to think much. I just wanted to get better. I thought I could get better.

A few months later, another ER visit for pain I can't control or understand. But during this visit, I am met with suspicion. I can tell the doctor and the nurses think I am saying the pain is worse than it is, that I am faking it. Now there's anger on top of embarrassment. Pair that with the chronic pain and anxiety, and I just want to scream or disappear.

Don't doctors chart these things? Can't he see my history? Why am I having to prove anything? I can't fucking walk!

3

During my twenties, the symptoms kept coming, and I kept explaining them away.

Until I couldn't.

I was in a warm pool, physical therapy again, as if I were injured and going to get better. I felt like I was getting better. I was still only taking the meds when I absolutely had to and then not always. The mother of another patient was there often at the same time I was, and she would talk to me. I would answer. I was nice, but I wasn't very talkative. One day, she heard the PT tell me I needed to use the medication to relieve the pain, use it regularly, blah, blah. I wasn't really listening to this twenty-something-year-old girl. I just continued my water ballet. After I was done, the mother of the other patient said, "I don't mean to be rude, but . . ."

I hate when people say this because you know they are about to be very rude.

She said, "I am a nurse, and I feel the need to tell you something. I see you here often. I can tell you are in terrible pain. I also hear the physical therapist talk about you not taking your pain medication."

She continued because I was actually listening to her for some odd reason, "You can do what you want with your body. I don't know your history, but I see you. I see the scar the entire length of your spine, and I see the swelling, the pain you are in. If you are being given medication, there is a good reason. To get your pain under control, you take the medication daily. Then you never have to get to the point where it's completely out of control. That is what people don't realize about medication, with chronic conditions that are not going away. Medication will keep it under control enough for you to function better day by day. It will help. Gradually you adjust to it."

"*Who does this bitch think she is?!*" I thought to myself. I was still listening though, and I was not sure why. It's funny who can affect you when you least expect it.

If anyone else had attempted that, I think I would have told them to mind their own fucking business. But she got to me—that or I just needed to hear it from someone on the outside looking in. She was just a stranger, she knew little about me.

All it took was for someone to say "Stop fighting."

I cried like a baby after she left. I knew I was going to be different. My body was going to get worse, I was going to have to try to do something other than ignore it. You can't win if you're fighting your shadow.

And so it began. I accepted the medication in a way that allowed for some relief—or allowed for me to numb the pain long enough to hurt myself a bit more by feeling a tiny bit better and getting out to socialize or work and then being hit with another avalanche of pain reminding me quickly where I stood. My body, this pain inside me was deciding my days now. My mind had no say. All days were planned around how to get through with constant pain.

It's infuriating how impossible it is to be normal, to try to interact with normal people. Even just sitting and having a conversation is hard when all you have on the brain is pain. It permeates everything everyday. Trying to be around others and exist can be exhausting. I can't not focus on it and I'm always detached. I'm not present. But I can either live with it around others or live alone.

Either way, when I was out of answers for how to deal with my body, and when I wasn't even asking questions, someone gave me an answer that made sense to me.

Medicate the beast. *Tame* the beast. It's not going away.

4

I gave recovery an arbitrary time limit. In a few months, I thought I would be better.

A few months later . . . I am taking medication at a rate that alarms me.

How can any of this happen?

Who am I?

I have some good days. I love it when I feel like it's a good day. But then, it's a good day compared to what? To lying in bed or on the sofa, feeling my muscles atrophy? When you have damaged your lower back beyond repair, you cannot sit or walk or stand without feeling some version of the symphony of pain. When you have destroyed the nerves that supply blood to your feet, this is obvious in each step, every time I stand still for a minute, or even less. The sensation is a mix of pain and tingling with fire and itchy hate. I must immediately put my feet up. It's all day. Driving around to run errands now requires breaks where I must put the seat all the way flat. Lowest points in life come when sitting and standing are impossible in a variety of ways, and I have to continue to do EVERYTHING, EVERY DAY because if I stop for too long, I may never get up again. That's too scary to imagine. So, I move as much as possible.

Very often I think there is no point in going down this road. Living in pain is living in hell. Medication is doing nothing but adding some nausea and dizziness to the mix.

I feel angry or anxious. How can I accept that my body is taking me prisoner? Paralysis? Whatever the name, it is a slow, mean, relentless, sneaky, dick-faced bastard.

HELLO I'LL BE STEALING FROM YOU TODAY

I was once a dancer, taking multiple classes a week for years and throughout college. My body was stiff, but I could do it. I could move and jump and dance and feel free. I loved to ride roller coasters and go to the beach, go on vacations full of activity with my family. My friends and I were always busy, in college especially. I was a student, an actress working in commercials and some films, a bartender. I traveled with my friends when I could afford it.

I had been wasting my time trying to figure out what was wrong, and it was there looking me in the mirror each morning. I was growing old too fast, looking like I was hurting, feeling like I could not walk some days. I can't walk, but I want to fucking dance. How can I come to terms with this?

I still wake up and have hope that things will change, that it won't forever be like this. My ability to walk through life without thinking about each step, my laugh, my dreams for shit that could happen—all of it is still here.

I dream inside this horrible, anxiety-filled, scary stillness of my own body. I don't know this body anymore. It's a body that does not move at all while I sleep. I must use props to find a certain level of comfort and go to sleep with pills that can knock me out, away from this bullshit. When I wake, I feel the stiffness in all the joints and my spinal bones crushing nerves. The medication has worn off, and I'm left wondering if it's worth trying to turn over and grab more pills or just try to go back to sleep. I usually cannot go back to sleep because I'd have to swallow more shitty pills.

My degenerative diagnosis is stealing from me. I've wasted too much time, gave too much time to unimportant shit. Now I'm getting robbed of my future self. My mind is telling me the way out is to just sleep forever, to stop hoping this will get better. Then a morning will come where I can move a bit, and I just want to fucking live. To walk, to cook, to eat at restaurants, to visit friends, to go places and not have to plan around my daily limit of energy output. I'm eager to get better but afraid to think that it's possible. Each time I allow myself a second to think it, I get knocked down again.

    The worst part is no one knows, will ever really know what this is actually like. I try to hide it, the symptoms they can't see and I don't speak of. I don't have to say I'm hurting. Most people in my life can tell by looking at me, but they will never truly understand this type of bodily breakdown. I couldn't have imagined the severity of this just a year ago while it was happening to me. So, there is no possible way anyone else can know. No one could ever get it because if they did, they would have to be in it, and they aren't. It's consuming, it reaches inside of you, and it takes everything. I am not able to be a good friend, and it's hard to even talk to anyone about regular-life shit when my world is caving in. No one wants to hear that, and I don't want to tell anyone. So I cut myself off more. It's anxiety due to pain. It's depression due to the anxiety of being stuck inside of my own pain. It's every second of every day thinking about this negative part of my life, a huge part. I am stuck inside of me, the one place I've been trying to escape for years.

5

A woman, who feels like a girl in soul and an old lady in body, stands on the balcony of the fourteenth floor of her favorite beach condo. Some of her biggest life moments have taken place here. Her last ten years revolve around this beautiful view. And now . . . the boy, two years old, adores it too. The love she feels for the beach and the boy are pure and intense, just like the pain that ravages her body.

She wears a red cape-like dress, and the boy asks, "Mommy, are you Superwoman?"

She smiles at the lovely boy, who really thinks she is Superwoman, and she wishes she could be that.

Then suddenly, she wants to jump. Off this balcony and onto the hot concrete, flying like Super Mom. Then he could always remember her as strong, as flying, and never see her breaking down. She loves him too much to allow him to watch her hurt. But she wants to watch him grow, too.

Her love for him wins.

6

After years, I have now come to a place in life where I look at my days and I think . . . what the fuck? How did I get here? My days are so mundane at times—wake up, breakfast, errands, cleaning, pain, meds. Taking care of my son is the absolute highlight of the day.

When I was trying to get pregnant, I was aware of the increasing pain I felt inside myself. But I wanted it, and I wanted him. Having him keeps me going, but up until I became a mom, I had years of slowly falling apart. He helped me feel better about my life, but the pain isn't going away. And now I have to consider the effect my pain will have on him. Will I be able to care for him?

I often wonder where the hell I would be right now if not for him. Would I have run away? Again? Would I have just taken off for a year or more, just disappeared into a crowd somewhere halfway across the world?

I sometimes wanted that—to run, just be away from everything and everyone. Yes, the day-to-day pain would not go away, but the awful realization that my life is not quite what I wanted would be a lot less severe. I could just fly away, go wherever the wind takes me. Stop this relationship I am in and take off. Give him the freedom to find a new love. Give myself the freedom of a guilt-free life, and the weight of my relationship could be lifted from my shoulders. I could take off and just live. Find a sex-free life partner, someone to spend time with and travel with and split bills with and then help each other. No pressure of a relationship. But here I am, and my life remains as it has for months now. Now that my

HELLO I'LL BE STEALING FROM YOU TODAY

son is here, I can't run away, but . . . if it were just me in this life . . . I don't know.

My husband and I are trying to figure out our lives together. He wants us to be a couple, and I want . . . I don't know what I want exactly, but I know somewhere along the line, the sexual desire in our space has decreased and become almost nonexistent. However, I love him, so it's confusing. Knowing him, being in a relationship with him almost all of my adult life makes it even more confusing.

Now we have a son, so I stay in the relationship because I don't know what is the right thing to do there is. He needs us both each and every day. He loves us both because we are with him all the time. He knows that and feels secure. Changing that could really make him doubt everything he knows so far to be true and to be real. I don't want that, so I have to try my hardest to give both of them the life they want and deserve without completely sacrificing myself and my wants and needs in the process. These had been the happiest last few years with the birth of my son through circumstances that I thought at times were impossible . . . but now the feeling has slowly changed, and that has been so very hard. I am still so happy I have my son, but do I have the strength to fight to keep a relationship together? Is that good for any of us?

It's awful how life can be so silly and deceptive. You get the most beautiful creature who you want to love in the best way, and at the very same time, you get so much doubt about the union that created him. How is this fair? Can I train my brain and my body to respond correctly? Is that possible? Or will I have to force myself to go through the motions, make the sacrifice? I am hearing this more and more . . . just having sex for the sake of the relationship, not because you want it. Lots of adult women have told me this, and in the same breath have told me they are happy. How? Do people know how to be happy? Why would we stay in relationships that don't work? Are we that afraid?

Can't we be adults and know it can't always last forever?

At times, I think the sexual abuse as a child led to some of my pulling away from my own sexual feelings or desires. I did not want to be touched by anyone at a certain point, and that can be due to my past or my present issues. Pain, anxiety, medications, phobias, and physical exhaustion at present. Childhood issues of abuse and the surgery I had so young in my past. My whole life leads me to want to isolate myself completely. The relationship isn't working and it's hard enough to get through days, just caring for myself and my son. Seeking isolation at times because I cannot take any more of the arguing. Along with overwhelming pain and anxiety and exhaustion, it's too much. Too much for anyone to take on. I'm not sure exactly when it began . . .

It started slowly at first.
Detachment.
Feeling unsure.
Less attracted, less attractive.
The smell was off, and smells matter so much.
She felt it.
She fought it.
Blamed herself for it all.
Until that fall . . .

Only so much you can do to stop your own mind
   Your own body
   From drifting
   Drifting slowly away from what you know
   Or what you thought you knew
   It's not sudden.
   It's not a choice.

HELLO I'LL BE STEALING FROM YOU TODAY

Just a tiny whisper of an inside voice
Saying "No, it's not the same!"
Look !
Listen!
See!
Pay attention to me!

7

The vows, that's where we really screw up. Vows are strange. Marriage, relationships, all of it is so full of unintentional lies. There are some intentional lies, but I'm talking about those subtle ones we don't think will be lies—promising to always love another person you think you know very well.

It's hard to love ourselves at times, and it's never going to be possible to promise to feel the same way about ourselves ten years from now, much more anyone else. We get older, and usually we question who we even are, so how can we claim to know another person inside and out if we don't even know ourselves? It's hard to say. It's hard to do.

There will be a day—it could be years from now or just moments away—where you will look with wonder at this person you thought you knew. You will see some new face they've never shown you or that you tried to ignore. Either way, it will come out, and you will be shocked to find that you don't know this person. Your feelings will change.

We all have two faces, and we often show those closest to us the worst one. This is reality. So why don't marriage certificates expire? Maybe every ten years or so, you would really have think about if it was working out. Have you grown together or apart? Who are you? Who is this person? Do you even care anymore?

And why is it that someone always has to be the victim, the wronged party? When do people realize that it takes both to break a bond? It happens slowly, and you hear the words and see it breaking down, but you choose to ignore it. It would be better if we could all realize that we are actually fucking human beings with beating hearts, who love and don't want to be dicks. Well, most of us. If we all just accepted that things change, people change . . . We just never know if we will change together or if our changes will drive us apart. It's not a question of fault. It's reality.

If my husband looked back at our time together from the perspective of WE, I think he would see a fairer picture of what happened. Right now, he is thinking everything that goes on between us is happening to him, like he is not part of it. We have both been here, in this, all these years. At times, it's me doing something he doesn't like. Other times, it's him. And there are so many cases over the years when he was absolutely frightening. It's hurtful when he talks to me as though he hates me. I think that's the worst, when you are with someone for years and you trust them and then suddenly, they show a hateful face, a face you don't deserve and don't recognize—don't *want*.

Over the past couple of years, it's like I can't breathe sometimes. If we are arguing all of the time, I am always watching what I say, not able to be me, not able to just breathe. I feel like I don't express what I want to say and just end up holding it all inside. There are only so many things a person can hold inside before they just blow up. Even when I do talk, try to say what I feel, I am not heard. So I just shut up. Shut him out.

It's not all bad, though the end of something feels that way. But our lives have been spent together. Almost all of my adult life was spent with him, and we were often happy.

Love is a story, and some stories are long and others are short. We have been lucky ours was long, and we still want to be in each other's life. But how we will fit into the lives of each other is up to us. Drop the anger, both of us. Take time away, both of us. That is the only way we will heal. Not this being in the same room with each other but not talking—that is not time away. We need time to unlink the emotional chains—the ones in our souls, our hearts—and take care of them, polish them.

Stop being a victim. Start trying to move forward into something we can be, together, into a way to communicate where we can both speak and be heard.

Say words. Listen to words.

Change with it, and it will be easier for everyone. Fight it, and it will always be a fight, and one day someone will wake up with that other face on, walk into the kitchen, and say, "Get the fuck out of here and don't come back." Or we can grow up, grow old, move on, maybe date other people. Whatever happens.

But if we handle it right, we will still be that old couple sitting in our rocking chairs looking at the beach, having a cocktail and talking about the old times. We don't have to throw it all away.

8

My life is filled with these little contradictions that are counterintuitive. But they are present most days . . .
 Meditation . . . medication.
 Yoga . . . yelling.
 Breathe . . . berate.
 Love . . . loss.
 Everything . . . nothing.
 The difference between what I say and what you hear is so extraordinary!

I cannot expect anyone to fully understand me, what I go through daily, just as I don't expect to fully understand others. But there is a language of kindness that we once understood and that is now lost. Too many misunderstandings pile up, and one day you can't find your way back. But the way your words come out, the way your actions are, you can't see what I am seeing. You are doing what you say I do. You do something, and then say I do it. It's a cycle I don't want to be in. And if I let it, it could make me insane,

I asked over and over for peace and understanding. I am getting accusations, and peace only comes if things go exactly as you orchestrate.

Once again we are here, but no one wants to talk about it. Different reasons, same avoidance. It is so hard to do this when it comes down to it. There's never time for it, or it's always time. I just know that our lives are going to pass us by, and we are going to regret missing out on that time. We are just waiting for something—for different things entirely. This is not what it's supposed to be like.

It's time to change. For all of us.

So I have decided on the fucked-up, difficult path of most resistance. Wish me well!

9

I want to melt into someone, feel like I'm losing my breath and mind to another person . . . free!

I tell him this, and he says, "I am here. We have this together." Is he ever wrong? Not to him. But I know if it were there, it would have emerged by now. I'm cheated out of what I want to feel. He is cheated out of me. We're both are lying to ourselves, and neither of us want to say the words.

Why is it so bad to want to feel again? Both of us ask ourselves this, though about completely different topics and people and worlds.

Melt. Into. Someone.

To let go and know there will be a net. Is that so bad?

I wonder if my body still has the ability to feel that want, that pull towards someone attractive. This body feels so empty and so very numb.

"CHEATER."

The word was filthy, never described me. Cheating on spouse was a pastime left to the very wealthy or the stupid, not the normal happy people who knew each other for years and respected one another.

But . . .

At first it was like trying on a new skin—not sure, seemed kind of gross. But I could justify ideas once the new skin was zipped up. It made perfect sense to try at least. Otherwise, deny yourself the knowledge of it being a problem with you or the relationship.

Easy to justify when it was only an idea, but once it was

here, it was so different. It was sleazy and dirty, nothing familiar. Not gentle, not refined, raw. Just what I needed.

I woke up to my life. It was in order, but my head was a mess. Having dreams of the nightmare of cheating, of wanting, of losing it.

When you call, I will try to answer, say I am fine, laugh when prompted, haha, yes, of course . . . I am dying inside.

I wish I had known then, just how fragile, how fucking breakable, we all are.

10

Milestones . . . Like big birthdays, first apartment, first good apartment, first home bought and sold.

Then pain milestones . . . First time you started needing meds daily, first time you felt real nerve pain shoot through your whole body, first time your hands went blue, cold and numb in summer, and your feet lost feeling, first day you have to choose what you can do based on pain. Bodies atrophy. One thing brings down the next.

People don't get the pain others feel—the extent of it. They don't really believe it. They can't see it, it's so internal and personal, and most people in pain can hide much of it, so others don't understand or they think you are lying.

But meds are the only option at a certain point. Wanting pills. Wanting to feel like a zombie, only getting rid of some of the pain. I fought that for a long time, further hurting myself, calling new pains "injuries that might go away." At physical therapy, that nurse helped me understand meds better, but I will never be comfortable with taking this shit.

Pharmacy staff can be the worst, making you feel like you are insane and on pills for pure pleasure. Fuck you. Who do you think you are, judging me for taking medication I need in order to get out of bed? The medicines *you* sell to people?

There are no walks or events to support those with this random assortment of pain that will never go away.

Maybe because there is no cure, never will be.

But there are some things about pain that I still find surprising—how much you can actually take, how long it can last.

It feels like the amount of pain I feel can't fit in this body

anymore. I fear living, and I fear death because I want to be with my family. I know a time could come when I can't stand or walk, and that makes me feel like I have no reason to go on. I take strong medication, and the pain is so much stronger.
No one knows.
No one will ever know.
I can't explain what my life has become, and I don't know how to stop it from taking over.
I need better days, good days.
Life is not meant to be lived in pain. How can I hurt this much all the time? I deserve to feel better. It still surprises me that I think it could get better someday. I want to think that. I have to.
Life should be more under my control. I have no control. The only comfort is my bed—I am alone in it and will be for a long time. I am most comfortable physically, yet I am emotionally drained and so alone. I feel the need to be alone. How much this affects my brain scares me and scars me.
I want to love my life. All of it.

11

I recognize the passing years by the growing number of drugs on my nightstand and my increasing inability to function.

The reality of my never getting better came in waves over a couple of years. Slowly, I did less, spoke less, cared less, felt less. I was trying to find ways to heal something that could not be healed. Many of my friends did not understand why I never answered my phone: I couldn't talk. I just had no energy to attempt normal life, and conversations seemed unimportant. I missed my life, and no one could really understand or see it. The few people who did come around knew some of the difficulty, as much as they could at least. I went into a hole of pain, anxiety, and fear, far away from everyone that I knew but felt so detached from.

Each day I attempt to do more.
When my body is tired I ignore.
Not sure when I started to think this way.
That every single thing had to be done today
It's the pain growing along with the denial and fear.
I am a robot pushing away feelings
With a smile for my son
But no sympathetic ear.
I'm walking alone in this world because I am me
On my path, walking too fast to really see
Life is happening each day outside these walls.
But I rarely care because going out adds more
More to do and more to plan and try to fucking care.
I need to walk.
I need to run.

I need to fly.
If I stop, I die.
That's my reality, it's what's in my mind.
Seek chaos and chaos you shall find.
I want to start over again, alone and away. I feel lonely though and long for connection, to someone who gets me, a new person. I need new something, a location, people, all if it.

12

I can escape into my imagination at times, creating stories about other people who live inside of my brain to amuse myself.

I'm pretty sure I have an inner gay man . . . or at least an idea of who he would be right now . . .

I love the intimacy gay men get to have with girls, I would totally be the gay guy who girls walked around naked in front of, and I would be hands-on with my lady friends in a nonsexual way—more in the interest of the woman's body as a beautiful, odd mess.

I like the gay man witty banter, and I know I'm generalizing here, but everyone's interpretation is different, after all. The gay man inside of me would be quick with the funny comeback, putting you down in a loving way.

My inner gay self would be wildly social, like dinner-party-with-nameplates type social. I would host small dinner events, some themed, that my friends would all want to attend, but I would have to invite people according to their personalities.

My inside gay man may even rarely date men, opting for a wealthy life partner who only needs someone to share a life, not a sex life. This leaves me open for all sorts of trouble and many stories!

I would be well-schooled and well-traveled and maybe even expat some of the year, take myself on tour. And we are Pilates ripped!

This thought began as me thinking of myself sexually—where do I fit?

For a moment or two, I thought maybe I was gay. I find the female body much more beautiful than the male, but who doesn't? I had my moments of lesbianism, but it didn't quite fit either. I liked the touching and kissing of the girl, then CUT, bring in that one guy that knows just what to do to finish the job.

Later in life, I just decided I don't want to have sex anymore until I really want it. I won't do it just because I'm supposed to or because it's part of someone else's idea of a healthy relationship. I will just do what the fuck my body says. Listen to it.

I'm sure someday soon it will come alive and express itself in some way. Until then, I am not interested, too much baggage comes with that. I just want to see where I stand.

    I like this personality. I get to be intimate with women, be witty and social, spend money shopping and traveling, and free to be me—kinder, more personable, OPEN.

That's the big one. I don't open easily. I close many doors simply because I lack the nerve or energy to see what may be on the other side. Anxious people often want to be someone else. I could be a devious actress because I think I was born to wear a thousand different faces in my lifetime. I would love to allow another personality to take over mine—how freeing! Go inside the crazies, backstory them, understand their defects in personality, understand we are all defective—some just hide it better or try to be like everyone else so they don't raise suspicion.

    Now, I just need a gay-man-inside-my-body name, a good strong worthy name!

13

When I was young, my mom always wanted me to be more interested in family, closer to family. She thought I was too interested in my friendships, that her and the rest of my family were not as important. But my friends knew me in a different way. We had chosen each other. I could talk more openly about subjects I found interesting and feel more comfortable doing it. I felt like you could have friends while appreciating family, but my mom made me feel as though I was doing something wrong, unacceptable.

Later in life we would both realize we were wrong. You can't have just family or just friends. If you expect your family to fill in the holes, you can end up very lonely. Everyone is busy. Life is busy. Being family does not make anyone anymore available.

Relying on people is setting yourself up to be let down, so you have to find people who fit and then appreciate them consistently. It's hard to find people you want in your life, so if you can, it's important to hold onto them and nurture those relationships. It's too hard to go through life without good relationships, wherever they come from.

Otherwise, there is loneliness, and life feels empty. Family is not enough, and friends are not enough. You need a balance, a circle of people who get you and you can be yourself around.

I lack this.

14

Hello, panic.

I think my therapist is judging me . . . No, I know my therapist is judging me!

She asks open-ended therapist questions, and my answers are things like:

My panic attacks make feel like I am drowning in a pool of filthy water, and I can see the surface but can't quite get to it. Sometimes, at the checkout line in a large store, I feel like I am in hell. I can't stop listening to all the loud noises or looking at the strangers around me. They may be perfectly nice or perfectly crazy, but this is just what anxiety makes me feel like in that situation.

Her answer will be something about my use of "filthy water" and "filthy people," and why do I think I am so focused on that?

You're the therapist. How about you give that one a shot?

Or another thing I find myself telling her because I have no edit button today:

I have sat in waiting rooms, looking around, wondering how fucking ignorant some of my fellow waiting room drones really are, the really bad ones. I hear their mind-numbing cell phone conversations, and I at times want to stab them. I also watch them treat their children like shit, and I want to rip out their eyeballs and shove them down their throat. Then, there are their dirty fingernails . . . don't ever think they have been cleaned. It drives me batshit loony bird to sit still surrounded by fucking stupidity and meanness!

This is usually when I feel the judgment creeping in. I

thought therapy was about opening up, saying the things we can't normally say out loud? No? Did I get this wrong?

She doesn't even help me or try to help me. She gives me printed-out forms on dealing with anxiety!

Really, this will be great. Why didn't I think about just taking deep breaths? Thank you, printout!

Before I leave her office one day, I tell her:

Some days I just panic about life in general and what my reaction might be. What if someone tried to take my child? Or what if someone tried to touch him in an unwelcome manner or just fucks with him in general? I would have to murder someone. That would be awful! I could hire a person dressed as a fun character kids like, maybe the mouse, and go to school and corner the bullies and grab their nuts and say, "Fuck with [Insert your child's name here.] again, and you're dead, fucker!"

She says that we will deal more with that in our next session, and maybe I need to work on my anger issues. Your tone isn't doing much to inspire me to do that right now, though!

I do not go back to her. She gave me no new knowledge during my time there, and that's just bad business. I also doubt there are words that will change my thought process. Just a kind person to talk to would be okay. She was a handshaker anyway. I distrust those people in general.

15

Through all the times we have almost purposely tried to push the boundaries of life and death, through the shit we pulled our bodies into and out of, the tight group of friends remained. Insane, but alive and well for the most part. We had gone to the edge and back too many times and now were settled into a routine of careers, kids, business owners, etc. Most of us keep in touch, and every now and then we get together and try to be crazy or talk about just how crazy we once were.

Then an old friend from our core group of friends in Nola, a friend for years who made it through all the cocaine-fueled nights, long days of drinks and drugs, road trips while fucked up, all this and more, suddenly and tragically died. During a night out, at a bar we had all gone to hundreds of times. An accident happened. No one can wrap their brains around it.

He was on the balcony, about eighteen feet up, drinking—but grown-folk drinking, nothing crazy. And he fell off the balcony onto the road and sidewalk, onto concrete, straight on top of his head, just like that. He bled immensely at the scene and had hours of surgery to relieve pressure and remove blood, tubes coming out of his head. None of us knew what to think. We had all done things that could have killed us so many times, but this freak accident took him so fast. A day later, he couldn't fight any longer and died on New Year's Eve. How could this happen? We all thought about our group, the things we did to our bodies for so long, the chances we all took, and we made it through that. Then he just fucking died, fell on his fucking head. It's so unfair.

Right then, I no longer wanted to die. I wanted to get myself better, the best I could. I wanted to make a happier life, even with the pain, and I wanted to connect with all of my friends again. I no longer wanted to hide. I wanted to understand that life is a gift. I wanted to really know that.

So, at that moment, I vowed to study meditation, yoga, health, anything to make my days better.

Because any one of us can just fall on our fucking heads at any moment and then what was the point of all that moping around, feeling sorry for what you don't have? What is it all for?

If anything can be learned from tragedy, it's that life is quick and scary. It will never be what you expect. So I just need to find a way to be happy with what I have right now.

Celebrate something . . .

Love. Celebrate love and just realize that though I made it through my roaring twenties, there is no guarantee I will make it across the street tomorrow.

My body pain will be here, so either I can learn to live a happy version of me or sulk around through my days.

I decide then to find the version of me who recognizes the beauty in life. Finally I know something that I feel is worth knowing.

It's out of my control, and that's okay because it has to be.

16

Time has gone by. I still have to elevate my cold, blue, dead feet and lay my back down flat instead of sitting and curl up on my side to change things, but I refuse to stop moving.

I felt myself slipping away, the pain and the medication taking me to Anxious Lazy Town, where I want to do nothing and say, "Why me?" But fuck that, as long as I can use my body some parts of the day, I will. I have been trying to strengthen my body through exercise, bringing me, at the very least, a break and some joy. I have started to move more, swim, and walk. I can lie in the sand on the beach, and I can smile at that. I tried to reach out to friends again, open up as much as I can about what I'm dealing with and let them in. I even started to talk to a few friends about mundane shit, and it felt fucking fabulous! I miss myself and want some sort of life back.

I cry a ton for my time wasted. I think I should have been acting, not partying.

Acting: that little bird won't fly away. Acting is in me, no matter what the struggle. I had tried again, took some classes, booked some work in a few commercials, a few films. I didn't tell anyone on set about my pain, and I had been dead tired by the end. But I loved it that much.

There were a few sets I had to leave. The pain or panic was too much. I always made sure to burn no bridges and luckily had friends on the other side of the camera. But working on film sets for twelve-plus hours is hard for anyone, not just me. But it was harder for me, and I pushed that away too. I should have . . .

I should've, could've, would've . . . It is time to let go of that part of me that regrets. After years of being in the lowest parts of my psyche, I have found a higher place. I want to be better. I don't expect to be like I was in the past. This frees me to be delighted when something does make me feel better. Without expectation of change, the change feels so fabulous and welcomed. Some things still don't go so well, but you can't stay mad forever about things you can't change. It is okay.

17

Still the one thing I hate, HATE, is looking at progression through photos, modeling pictures, or photos with friends and family.

Through the years that this pain was taking over my life, I can see it in those faces of mine, a million subtle changes. The eyes don't lie, especially about pain or stress or internal struggles with illnesses. My eyes are always focused but not really there, far away, thinking of the things I just couldn't stop thinking about. Body pain. Fear. Illness.

Eyes of pain, slow and creeping into daily life.

Fear is coming slowly.

Eyes of cancer, fast changes.

Taking over my thoughts, my life, my world . . . I can see it.

PHOTOGRAPHS.

Today, I felt alone, sad, and unsure. I called an old friend, and within a few minutes, I realized that it's not what it seems, the lives of others. We all see those pictures with smiling faces, happy families, vacations, perfect days, and beautiful nights of other people in our lives. We see our own, too, and we know they aren't always true.

Behind the happy faces are often thoughts of anger or frustration. Seconds before photos are taken, we may hate the person who is smiling next to us. Our vacations look beautiful in still shots, but we may have been depressed, crying for a reason we hide. Seeing all these happy faces online, the websites we visit daily, and only seeing one side of things can fuck our brains up a bit, make us feel as though we are the only ones going through shit, walking daily in and out of uncomfortable madness and existing in a feeling of despair, wondering why we are not happy, why we are alone and hurting.

But no one wants to show that side, and we forget we are only seeing one angle. Seeing what people want us to see. It's nice to call a friend and vent about a failing relationship, having no family, and feeling alone . . . only to realize this is most of our realities. Happy, sad, anxious, in pain, wanting what you don't have, hating the person in your life, loving the person but not in the same way, losing siblings who are alive and well but dead inside, realizing you have only a few phone numbers to dial, moving forward. Things will be different tomorrow, next week, next year. But the one constant are the photos. They just keep smiling, and they LIE. Smile for the camera, scream in the car when you are alone.

Live this life the way you must with what you are given. But try to have friends to remind you that this is not only you, it's everyone. We all have our something, our exhausting matter at hand.

My life is hard right now—this I can see when comparing myself in photos—but I'm going to get through it because the few close people I have, they are really there. They have been for a long time, and I just couldn't see it until now.

18

Regret? No, I am who I am because of what I did and what I didn't do. I lived my life with a different set of rules, I had some fun, and some of it just taught me where I didn't want to be. Nothing broke me from my past. I am in this hell of pain because that's life. Some people get bone diseases, Rheumatoid arthritis, fibromyalgia, stenosis of the spinal column, discs bulging under the pressure from the others, nerves pinched and broken, and a dash of anxiety disorder. These things happen, like dominoes falling, once they get started, you can't stop them. One issue feeds the next and so on until it's so many things that there is nothing to be done.

It's just about daily choices at this point. What gets my energy today?

It's funny how when I was my healthiest physical self, if someone had told me all of this was coming, starting to build inside of me, I wouldn't have believed it. I knew something was wrong. I had hints, but I pushed those away just like I did the others. But to know it would have been this bad would have been impossible to imagine. Like I've said, it's just not possible to know what it's like until you are in it.

That may be a good thing. I would rather I had lived thinking I was fine, that I was just experiencing a bit of pain, the type that came with dancing for over twenty years. It was better not to know these things were coming. If I had known, I would have limited myself or held back. I might not have taken trips out of the country at a moment's notice, driven through Mexico for days not knowing where I was going, flown to Hawaii feeling not quite right and then having a fucking blast surfing and eating fresh fish. Maybe I would have turned down opportunities that shaped me. So it's all okay. What is in my past goes with me wherever I shall go, and I will keep all of it.

19

Looking back through the eyes of adult me in the light of day at the bar we spent so much time in when we were kids is almost painful. It was always a popular dive bar, but it just seems so very sad that we spent so much of our life in this place. Was this fun? Being together was fun at times, but most nights ended in some kind of drama. Some nights ending in couples arguing or a drunk friend unable to walk, ending in tears, regret, wondering where else I could be. The next day, back to the life I knew.

It was a habit. When we were younger, it was partying to excess and talking about being artists, being whatever the fuck we wanted to be, but never going out and really being those things. I'm glad I made friends like those, but I know I could have left for a year, more even, and come back to the same thing.

I had an inner voice telling me then to go away the right way. "Move to the place you always wanted to be because you are an actor. You write plays. You danced for years, and you've been an actor since you can remember." I heard that voice, talked about it with a few people. But I didn't push it. I pushed into the Southern life, Nola life, hoping the acting jobs would come there, knowing even if they did, I probably wouldn't be able to get my ass up and to work. It was easier to say fuck it. Call myself an artist, a broken dancer, a struggling actress, a student—titles that made me feel better about doing nothing when I can clearly see now where I needed to be.

Life teaches lessons, gives us clues. If we are ready to hear those, we can do what we are meant to do. It seemed fun at the time, but did I just recall the fun and ignore the bad? Did I really see those clues?

The arguing from the nights before were not given a second thought the next day. The next day, we'd talk about the good stuff, the fun stuff, make it better in our memory.

But it wasn't great, and it's not too late to shake this shit up.

20

Looking back at us all, just childlike versions of our future adult selves, I'm struck by how many things stay the same. Time passes, we grow older, and we change. But who we were back then is who we still are now. We don't have the time to go out or the energy to party all night, but if we did, we would quickly see those old patterns emerging.

The ones who get drunk at every single get together even if it's a daytime, "fun," social event—they will still always get drunk. These are also the meaner ones, some rude to everyone, others rude in specific ways. The way they talk to people they are friends with once they are drunk, talking down to people one minute and then the next thinking nothing of it. We are like family, a bit nuts. Every family has its crazier ones. However, it is not okay, was never okay. You can't call someone a bitch one day, tell them to fuck off because you are drinking, and then say "Oh, I'm sorry" the next. This is not okay now and wasn't then, but we were too young to say.

They fall right back into the pattern. But some of us see this now and know it's not going to be accepted. That is no longer our reality. We are grown. We have new roles. We put our younger personality away, try to get rid of it as we grow, but much of it will follow us forever. The adult versions of those kids who thought they knew everything now know that we know nothing. We accept that life is crazier than we were, and most now try to live it the right way. We dysfunctional, loyal kids were just lucky through all the bullshit and now are adults who have moved away or moved on.

Many of us are going to remain close, and this is obvious

in how many people came together for our friend's sudden passing. We were all just kids in a city that many people get lost inside of or where they get sucked into something dangerous. We found a home in each other, and there we feel safe to be ourselves, flaws and all.

The happiest of the group seem to be the girls, and most are now single. They describe being single as the best thing they could have done—being single is salvation! What I'm going through is hard, but most of them are on the other side of it, and they like it much better there. However, most of us carry around guilt. Useless but heavy, guilt weighs us down. It makes us think we need to be something someone else wants rather than just being happy. But if we are living this life, with no idea when we could tumble off some balcony and die, then what are we fighting for if not happiness?

I've learned to that we must be good to each other, so the demons don't build up inside and all come out at once—yeah, that's a good place to start. Let go of grudges and things you can't control, and move forward. I've learned that saving a relationship that you have to fight for is not saving anyone. It's just an end to something that was. Learning to live after it is the trick. I'm learning from myself and my friends that at times I have been standing still, simply because I'm afraid to make a move, afraid to hurt anyone else. But why? That energy has to have a better place to go.

21

Maybe I won't ever really find myself or figure it out. Maybe I'm not meant to. This finding ourselves has gotten out of control. We don't have to know all the answers. It might just be okay to live life as it comes and know I have very little control over the big stuff. I fought with all my power to stop myself from crumbling, but I couldn't. I wasn't able to. I can pick the smaller stuff though. Use my energy controlling what to wear, what to do, who to do. I think about things that matter, let go of things that don't.

Some days are so beautiful I think maybe the pain will be okay. Some days, the pain is so severe I can't see any beauty. Maybe I won't be happy all day each day, but I bet I can always find happy moments.

Accepting that things won't get better with my body was the most freeing thing I ever allowed myself to do. It was hard and came slowly when I finally decided it was time to try to live some kind of life with this large bag of shit I have to carry around forever. Life can be a cruel, crazy ride. What we do, why we do it, where we end up—it's all a surprise. No plans work out. Something will rock your world when you think you are sailing along. This is the way it is. I finally understood I was not the cause of this pain, that it was genetic and the luck of the draw. This doesn't make it much easier. I still think of the what ifs . . . But I look around and see people who never leave their zip code, never try anything new, never move away, never stop being so fucking concerned with being normal . . . and I breathe a sigh of relief. I'm me.

For over ten years I struggled to get to a place where I

could grip onto my reality, my new me, and as my body gets weaker, the will to make the mind stronger has shown up to save me from myself. I have found my grip.

I know my only option is to live a healthy life but understand that this pain is forever, living with this pain is forever, and take it in completely. Accept it. Love the life I have. Like an old friend said, buy a ticket, take the ride.

Without this burden of pain, I may have never really gotten to the point of figuring out what I want or who I want to be.

I try to notice that now and accept my life as it is.

ACKNOWLEDGMENTS

Though not all true, these stories are based in truth. I am happy to say I am very close to both of my parents today, and have been for many years. We speak daily and they are my foundation in life, without them I don't know where I would be now. We have learned a lot from each other, and continue to grow together.

I would like to tell them how much I appreciate them for so many reasons. I thank them for having a daughter like me and choosing to understand me rather than judge me.

Thanks for the inspiration, dirty south! Louisiana has its blemishes but it remains one of a kind. Especially Nola, with the culture, the historical beauty, the very interesting cast of characters and the place I have felt most at home so far in my life. The south is original with an eclectic mix of people from all over the world, who are mostly Creole or Cajun, and all a beautiful mixture of races! I wish I had known of the historical importance of the town I came from at a younger age. I am glad I am learning. My friend Kevin, fellow bartender and all around intelligent southern historian, told me years ago. As I grow older and research my history I see he was almost exactly right. The day I met him he said 'brown freckles and green cat eyes, girl, you gotta be creole!'

Thank you to those people in life who inspire me for many reasons, and continue to surprise me with their strength and love . . . Alijah Sol, my heart and soul, Gayle, Wayne, Alex, Dodi, Megan, Jodi, LB, Hunter, and the friends I still have today. Thank you to the friends I had growing up, who helped me become myself and let me know it was ok to be myself.

ACKNOWLEDGMENTS

To my friend Hunter S Thompson, who saw in me more than I knew was there. A very good friend, crazy as hell, but good. The kind of person who can terrify and inspire within moments. I miss you.

For all of their time and patience with me, Adam and Christian at IRP. They both helped me immensely, challenged me often and I could not have done this without them. For my editors who worked on this puzzle of stories, and had such great input along the way, thank you!

Growing up, I was lucky to have three aunts who were like seconds mothers, Judi, Arlene, and Toni, thank you for your love and support. Also thanks to my cousins and my mawmaw and pawpaw (both sides of the family). You too, Uncle Pat!

If not for my beautiful son I may have not ever given myself the time to finish this project. Being at home with him day and night for years is a challenge and a gift. I did not have the gift of time, time to really sit and work. My work was him, always he was first. But I still was able to work on this manuscript during naps, and other small breaks during the day. When I put him to bed at night, I was exhausted, but I always worked for at least an hour. Usually many hours! Acknowledge the mothers who raise their kids while they work, while they try to do anything else, because being a full time mom is like having multiple full time jobs. I appreciate my time with him, it forced me to find an escape. My escape was looking into my past and creating something out of it. Watching a child grow is amazing, I am thankful for that time. I greatly appreciate what has come out of it also, a smart, happy, silly five year old, this book, and a new version of me.

I was helped along the way by test readers, and I appreciate all of the input from all of those who participated. I would especially like to thank Boisy, Christie, and my little Natty. You guys rock!

ACKNOWLEDGMENTS

All of the people we know will affect us in some way, some of these people will have a huge impact on our lives. My life was filled with people who came in, changed me, educated me, overwhelmed me, took me by surprise, empowered me, hurt me, made me see parts of me I didn't want to see . . . and then they were gone. They were all teaching me something, we do that for one another and it's important work. Notice the impact of others and appreciate it. Appreciate everything! It's possible to find good in even the worst situations. It's also possible to see the good in people if you choose to. We are more alike than we are ever going to be different.

Thank you writers who create stories that make us think, challenge us. Thanks to artists in general.

My sincere appreciation to the Chopra center for allowing me to grow a little, to learn more about meditation in my continuing quest to feel better and be better.

Acknowledgments can be very hard to write because so many thoughts and people come up in thinking about the past. So I say, if you took the time to acknowledge me on my journey through this life, then I too, acknowledge you.

www.ingramcontent.com/pod-product-compliance
Lightning Source LLC
Chambersburg PA
CBHW070609300426
44113CB00010B/1462